Encounter Builder

Reverend Amy Howard

with
Chrissy Kenerson
and
the Encounter Culture Team

Cover design by Timothy G. Moroz
Edited and interior by Rachel L. Hall, Writely Divided Editing & More

Encounter Builder / Amy Howard with Chrissy Kenerson. —1st ed.
ISBN: 979-8-9872953-0-4

Contents

PART 1: BUILDING YOUR ENCOUNTER WEEKEND

PART II: APPENDICES

PART III: SESSION NOTES

PART I

Building Your Encounter Weekend

Prologue

So, You Want to Build a Culture of Encounter...

Great! We're here to help. Encounters have been an integral part of our (Amy Howard and Chrissy Kenerson) lives for over 15 years of ministry, and as we look back over the years of friendships, conversions, healings and discipleship, we cannot imagine doing what we do as ministers of the gospel without the culture-building and equipping that Encounter weekends and Kingdom Ministry Training have provided. The two of us have collaborated to unpack and then package in what we hope is an accessible format exactly what goes on to plan and execute an Encounter Weekend, with the hope that just about anybody with the desire, a few friends, a little training, and a free weekend can host one of these life-changing events. The reason we dare to hope that just about anybody can do it, is because we did it... in the messiness of life, church, kids, jobs, successes, risks, and perceived failures. And for sure, it hasn't all been pretty, but I'm from New England, and if I'm being honest, if it's too pretty, I get skeptical. But before we get started, and in the spirit of a ministry which traffics in confession I want to share the following story.

True Confessions: Amy Howard's Encounter Story

I had a terrible first Encounter. I was just 23, fresh out of college, with a six-month old nursing baby in tow. Justin, my husband of not quite two years, came along, remaining behind in our room during the sessions to watch the baby. In the spirit of full disclosure, I didn't want to be there.

Encounter God Weekends are intended to be just that: *weekends* where, if one comes hungry, humble, and ready to be filled, one has a very real opportunity to encounter the living God. After 16 years of healing prayer ministry, I certainly can bear witness: the river rushes to the lowest place. Encounter Weekends are intended to help locate the low places—perhaps even create new ones—with the offer of bringing them out of the darkness and into the healing, hope-filled light of the Cross.

So, there I was: young, confused, skeptical, still hormonal from the last baby and in physical pain from a condition that wouldn't be corrected by surgery until later that year. I wasn't a great candidate for ministry, so I'm not particularly underwhelmed by the quality of my experience that weekend. I managed to find the one prayer minister who, I found out later, was in the throes of a particularly ugly divorce, and whose words to me when I tentatively went for prayer Friday night were, "You have a lot of pride, and you're going to have to get rid of it if you want God to do anything for you." Ugh—and quick aside—that's a great case study on how not to behave as a prayer minister! I still find it remarkable, considering my introduction to it, that this singular ministry weekend has become a mainstay in our discipleship culture so many years later.

Each weekend follows a general pattern of teaching, testimony, opportunity to receive prayer ministry, and—*repeat*. The central truth of an Encounter is that the ministry of John the Baptist preceded the ministry of Jesus: repentance leads the way for actual encounter with the living God. And often, the place of pain or sin itself become the liminal space of encounter. While we can be saved through our personal relationship with Jesus, as James tells us, our healing—our encounter—often comes from walking in the light with the church (see James, ch. 5). We have a large team of trained prayer ministers, all of whom have been to Encounter Weekends themselves, who all stand vulnerably before the cross and alongside their sisters and brothers. They all know that if you can call it sin, you can get set free from it.

I went home from my first Encounter without an Earth-shattering experience. There were no lights, or angelic visitations, or great burdens lifted. But I was deeply curious. I saw things that weekend that I had not come to associate with church. I witnessed testimony after testimony of people who, by my 23-year-old reasoning, should definitely be rocking in a corner somewhere, who were instead filled to overflowing with life, hope, and wellness. I listened to the stories of former prostitutes, cheaters, users, liars, victims of sexual abuse and trauma—things we didn't talk about in the churches I had attended. And these weren't only old conversion stories from 30 years ago; these were fresh, ongoing testimonies from the lives of new Christians, as well as those who had been walking with Christ for a half century or more. The testimonies came from lay people and church leaders alike. I watched something phenomenal take place amongst the participants: person after person took the plunge, and with the help of the prayer ministers, opened the dark, painful places in their souls to the healing light of God.

I grew up in church. No-go zones among different church groups I was exposed to varied from place to place, denomination to denomination: some didn't dance, some didn't drink, some didn't baptize their babies. One school I attended for three years forbade the use of face cards (weird, I know). But there was a universal, usually unspoken rule that everybody seemed to follow: you only confess your sins to God, never to another person. This was couched in Reformation language, when it was explained at all: we didn't need a priest to get to God. Therefore, confessing to God alone was sufficient. The only people who ever had to confess to anybody else seemed to be teen girls who got pregnant out of wedlock, and the results I remember from those episodes didn't leave the penitent with the glowing affects I had witnessed on the women at the Encounter Weekend.

I went home without an Earth-shattering experience, for sure—at least not the kind of shattering I could see, hear, or feel. As I write this, I realize that I was set free from the haunting shame of any number of secret sins that had kept me up at night which I confessed that weekend, despite my reticence and (yeah, sure) pride. What I did recognize after that first Encounter was a growing conviction that there was a link between the confession I saw, and the freedom that followed, and this did begin the slow deconstruction and re-imagining of some of my paradigms of community, and the effectiveness of the Gospel.

So I tried it out—the very next time I found myself in sin, I went and found a pastor and confessed, like we had done at the weekend. Some of you reading this are groaning right now, likely because you are older than 23 and have more life experience in the church than I had at that moment, and you have a good guess (probably within three) at what followed. Fortunately, I was not burned at the stake for my confession. I actually received what I have found to be a typical response of clergy over the years. The pastor looked a little startled, maybe a little embarrassed, and said something to the effect of "Oh, yes, don't worry, we all do that." Knowing what I had learned from the past weekend, I raised my eyebrows, dug in my heels, and responded something like: "No, it's sin. It's wrong. And I want to be set free." I proceeded to teach her the "4 R's" that the prayer ministers at Encounter had used to walk participants through their confession. And then I confessed again, coaching the poor pastor all the way. And lo and behold, God once again set me free. Free from the sin, free from the shame, free from the need to hide, and especially, free to love.

I like to live free. We embrace a radical, hope-filled honesty up here in the frozen North, and as a result, my best friends are the ones who can hear me rant, look me lovingly in the eye, and say, "That sounds like _____ sin. Would you like to get set free from it?" And then, even though I am now responsible for teaching the 4 R's to anybody who will hold still long enough, they will offer to walk me through them because they know that having a ministry of reconciliation is one of the central ways we manifest love one to another and is equally important for everybody, leader and lay person alike. I like to say that no matter how experienced I become at this thing, I still cannot cut my own hair in the back. We need each other.

My largest problem (not kidding here) is how many people—skilled, amazing ministers—would like to minister each weekend: there are always way more than I can book. They come, and they pay their own way just to be a part of what God is doing. Many more spend hundreds of dollars each year "paying it forward," sponsoring a weekend for friends, family members, and people of peace in their communities. We don't even do much to advertise the weekends. This is for two reasons. First, a personal encounter is a difficult thing to advertise because it varies so dramatically from person to person. And second, we don't really need to: peoples' faces do it for us.

And now, perhaps you are considering running an Encounter weekend. Maybe you've attended one and are ready to bring some of the healing and freedom you experienced to those around you. Maybe you're excited about the power of the Gospel and the opportunity to be encouraged watching the river run to the lowest places, transforming and renewing, convicting and healing. Maybe you're really looking forward to assembling a team who not only works together, but has the true fellowship of walking in the light together. Maybe you're a church leader who is ready to teach the whole body of Christ to do the works that He did and join you there. Whatever you're thinking, know that you are welcome. Come ready, leave changed.

You Don't Have to Be Special, You Just Have to Say "Yes": Chrissy's Encounter Story

"Will you teach me how to pray like that"? I finally asked my dear friend Amy Howard after once again witnessing her kindly and lovingly companion someone to Jesus through prayer. Amy didn't seem to mind how complicated or hurt the person was, she just prayed for whoever said "Yes" and those people encountered Jesus in a way that astounded me. She had a way of praying that seemed so real and tangible, like Jesus was her friend and she expected He would show up. I wanted to pray like that. More specifically, I wanted to know Jesus like that. After much coercion, Amy graciously agreed to meet with my sisters and I and teach us how to pray.

Our weekly meetings on the living room floor turned into times of confession and healing. We sat and learned about the love and kindness of God and the freedom He offers us when we confess to one another. It was a sweet and fruitful time. Amy kept mentioning that she had been ministering at Encounter Weekends in New Hampshire and we should really experience one for ourselves. Being the trusting lot that we are, we believed her and within a matter of a few weeks we had rallied 20 of our closest friends. We convinced them that it was important we take a pilgrimage from our reserved, Baptist roots of Levant, Maine and drive four hours south to a purely charismatic church in New Hampshire in order to experience complete strangers praying for us. Looking back on our approach now, we must have had the Lord's grace on our marketing strategy. I don't quite know why they all listened, but I am so glad they did.

***

With great anticipation and a few nerves we arrived at a ramshackle old building where the NH church that was hosting the Encounter Weekend. The front door didn't quite shut and the things inside the building were a bit out of order because they had just moved in a few days before our arrival. We found ourselves surrounded by boisterous, spirit filled women of all kinds. This was an entirely new experience, considering we were mostly Baptists. With the vast majority of our group having no previous experience with anything charismatic or any kind of prayer ministry, this was shaping up to be an interesting experience. We dove in and did all the things: we confessed, we cried, we prayed, we listened and shared and cried some more. It was uncomfortable, unusual, and at times chilly from the drafty front door, but the Lord was there and in that cold, chaotic room, the Spirit of God encountered a group of Baptist women, and we were changed from that day on. We came ready and we left changed.

I wish I could say that it was the awesome ministry team or the great organization or the beautiful facility that made the weekend so life changing, but that would not be true. I wish I could remember what I prayed about or who prayed with me or even the powerful stories of transformation I heard, but none of that stayed with me. I came home from that weekend with a greater freedom from the lies of the enemy over my life and a deeper love for the God calling me to walk in more fullness of who He created me to be. My life was marked by this event, but not just because of what I experienced in my own life. I watched my friends and family encounter God in a new and powerful way. They were now walking in more freedom and fullness than ever before. A desire began to build in me to bring Encounter Weekends to everyone who wanted to experience it.

I was 27 years old, had three babies three years old and under, I was building a house, helping plant a church and working in my family's business. I was not an ideal candidate to start a movement; I was not an ideal candidate to start anything. However, the Lord in His kindness allowed me to be a part of bringing this ministry to more people. Once we arrived home from that first Encounter Weekend, I began to dream about what it would be like if everyone in Maine had access to this kind of ministry. I wanted everyone to experience the healing and freedom of confession and receive the love and blessing of the Lord over their lives.

Our little team in Maine hosted our first Encounter about a year after attending our first Encounter. We were so excited to share what we had received with our friends and the excitement continued to spread. We continued to host these weekends and see lives transformed. Not only did the participants encounter God but the ministry team was equally impacted. I have never been part of a ministry that is effective on so many levels. The simple and powerful message of the Gospel is as true for the first-time participant as it is for the seasoned minister. It works every time.

This ministry formed the DNA of our little church plant. Confession, repentance, renouncing, releasing and receiving were our focus and we still do these simple but powerful steps every day with one another. It became a way of life. It formed our culture and our identity. Although years have passed and seasons have changed, those friendships and relationships forged in the fire of Encounter culture have stood the test of time. My closest friends are still the ones who will take the time to walk in the light with me and lovingly invite me to confess my sin and then go to Jesus together in prayer and receive healing. This is the power of the Gospel.

I know you are reading this manual and story because God has placed a desire in your heart for more. Something inside you is lit up by the idea that you could be a part of bringing healing and freedom to those around you. I want you to know that I believe without a shadow of a doubt that God is looking for people who will say *yes* to Him—people who are hungry for more of God and who are willing to partner with Him as He brings freedom and healing to those who have long been in bondage.

I am a very ordinary mom of five kids with a busy life and no special quali-fications to my name. You don't have to be something other than who you truly are to say *yes* to God and follow Him on this wild adventure. If you have hunger in your soul to see the Gospel go forth and willingness in your heart to say *yes* to God, you are ready. May God bless you with courage and faith as you take the next steps on this journey. I look forward to sharing stories with you of all the amazing things God will do through your *yes*.

A (Very) Brief History of Encounter Weekends

As you may have grasped from our stories above, Encounter Weekends didn't begin with us. The concept and skeleton framework are a product of revivals in South America. They began in Colombia in the context of the house church movement, which was spreading like wildfire. We're not sure who put the first weekend together, but we interviewed J. C. Alzamora, who was integral in their development, and also in teaching many ministers in the US about the necessity of not only preaching the gospel, but also spending real time in the process of helping people who have come to faith get set free from the bondage, sin, and addictions that are a part of their stories. J.C. and other ministers seeing many come to faith in South America realized early on that people could be "saved" and still really, really broken.

So they began a journey of establishing venues for deliverance and healing that would give men and women the opportunity to unpack where some of their pain and bondage was coming from, and also give them some tools to practically apply the work of Jesus Christ to their lives. There have been adaptations in various parts of the world over the past several decades, and it is our hope to provide the concise and communicable structure, clear teachings, ministry equipping, and leadership training necessary to make these life-changing events accessible to anyone, and then to assist church and community leaders in translating the dynamics of an Encounter Weekend into the normal lifestyle of their community.

A Guide to Your Encounter Guide

A quick guide to the guide you hold in your hands: This manual can be read in two different ways, depending on what you're up to this week (or month, or year). If your goal is to familiarize yourself with the overall ethos and project of Encounter Culture, and specifically, an Encounter Weekend, you'll want to primarily focus on the narrative section of each chapter. The narrative sections are distinguished with a plain background, and are usually not lists, charts, or financial breakdowns. If, on the other hand, you're working on establishing an Encounter Weekend sometime soon, and you're in the market for hard data, you'll want to pay attention to the sections with the gray background. These sections include all the technical data and are often accompanied by a blank corresponding worksheet in the appendix of this manual, which you can photocopy and reproduce to help you in your planning. If you have purchased a year subscription to *Encounter Builder*, you will be working through the gray sections and their corresponding appendix worksheets with your EC (Encounter Culture) coach over the course of a 12-month period, as well as unpacking your own personal journey, challenges, and growth throughout the process. It is our hope that with this manual and the support of our team here at Encounter Culture, you, too, can bring the beauty, intimacy, and power of the gospel to bear on your own community, church, family, and neighborhood.

May God the Father, God the Son, and God the Holy Spirit inspire you and fill you with great hope and courage as you embark on this new adventure in the Kingdom of God.

Questions for prayer and discussion:

1. How has my own experience (or lack of experience) of confession shaped my thoughts and feelings about confession?

2. Are there ministries, churches, or other Christians I need to forgive before I move into a new season? Consider possible internal vows or judgments you may still hold (for example: "I will never do church the way I saw it done;" or "I need to control the way others perceive me, either inside or outside the church, and it limits my ability to creatively and freely follow God's leading").

3. What are my initial fears, insecurities, or hesitations when it comes to the idea of engaging Encounter weekends on a deeper level?

4. Homework: If you have not yet attended an Encounter Weekend, sign up for one near you. Invite a core group of friends to join you as you experience this catalytic event together. Let your friends know that you're prayerfully exploring running an Encounter, who you are hoping to reach, and why you've asked them to join you.

Notes

Notes

Vision and Mission

WHAT MAKES AN ENCOUNTER WEEKEND an Encounter Weekend? In other words, if you are attending, ministering at or hosting an *Encounter Culture* Encounter, what should you be able to expect? What are some of our goals as we go about sharing the love and freedom of Jesus through the vehicles of Encounter Weekends and Kingdom Training?

Encounter Culture exists to bring the things that hurt to a God who heals, and help you discover who you were meant to be. We want to partner with God for the transformation of the culture of individuals and communities through teaching, prayer ministry, community creation and nurture, and developing biblical practices in order to foster authentic encounter with the Living God. If you are participating in, or running an Encounter Culture Encounter Weekend, you should be able to expect:

Consistent culture
Our culture is formed by a community who minister out of their own continual experience of encounter with Jesus, confession, healing, and love. We are passionate about intentionally preferring the "other" by using language and expression that is accessible, not "insider."

Safe ministry
Safety comes through confidentiality, accessible language, predictable form, solid and clear leadership structure, and sound tools.

Clear process
How to register, how to engage, and what the next steps are that you can take to stay involved, share the weekend with others, get trained, or join our ministry team.

Relational accountability
Encounter Culture is a ministry of the Anglican Diocese of New England. Though not particularly denominational in form or expression, we are ministerially submitted to our board and our diocesan leadership.

Accessible materials
The training manual, Kingdom: Living in the Presence of the Future, is available for purchase online, and other material is available upon request.

Trained ministers
Our ministers are themselves always recipients of ministry first and are available to help apprentice and train aspiring Encounter ministers.

We have cultivated specific tools for discipleship:

Encounter Weekends
At Encounter Weekends, we establish a paradigm for a life filled with radical, yet safe, authentic vulnerability, transformation, and encounter with the Living God.
Kingdom Training
Over eight weeks of Kingdom training, we work personally with you and your team of prayer ministers to bring this same, powerful, ongoing lifestyle to your congregation, your family, and your community.

At Encounter Weekend and Kingdom training, we strive to free, equip, and empower the *entire body of Christ* to be a conduit of Holy Spirit love and ministry to each other and within their respective spheres of influence.

We welcome leaders of all stripes and skills to engage in our ongoing monthly coaching cohorts. We also offer regular "going deeper" events to the community for continued skill development, community building, and personal healing.

Encounter Culture Vision:

To see people set free by the power of the Holy Spirit and released to walk in the fullness of their identity and mission as people created in the image of God.

Mission:

Encounter Culture exists to bring the things that hurt to a God who heals and help you discover who you were meant to be. As such, we are always working to refine the ways in which practice the following:

Safety in healing	To provide a safe setting where people can begin to experience the freedom and healing of confession
Equipping the entire body	To teach and train the entire body of Christ as prayer ministers equipped to bring the good news of the gospel through prayer to their own families, churches, and friends
Establishing paradigms of excellence	To establish paradigms of excellence in the areas of healing prayer, prophetic ministry, and deliverance ministry.
In-person and live online teaching	To equip Christian leaders throughout the body of Christ in the leading of their own vibrant prayer ministries, by means of online and in-person teaching, coaching, and written material, in order that they might become confident and responsible overseers, teachers, and practitioners of deliverance, healing, and prophetic ministry.

Coaching leaders	To virtually coach leaders while they lead their own Kingdom equipping sessions, apprentice aspiring prayer ministers leading up to and throughout Encounter Weekends, and to assist leaders in establishing local communities which pursue lifestyles of freedom, healing, confession, and vibrant ministry.
Networking ministers	To establish a network of trained and relationally-submitted prayer ministers who are able to serve the body through prayer ministry and local Encounter weekends.
Telling the story	To tell the story of God's greatness through personal testimonies of the transforming power of God's love
Growth	To grow in our identity as sons and daughters of God through experiencing God's love

Questions for prayer and discussion:

1. What do I feel like God is saying to me in this season regarding: A) My calling in His Kingdom? B) My growth in intimacy with Him? C) My community?

2. What aspects of Encounter Weekends capture my imagination?

3. List some examples of ministry "insider" language. Write out three reasons why it is important to avoid insider language whenever possible.

4. Homework: If you have not already done so, sign up for an upcoming "Kingdom Ministry Training," and invite your core team to join in as a site, or join another site in your area.

Notes

Notes

Laying the Foundations for Running an Encounter Weekend

THE NUMBER ONE FACTOR in laying a solid foundation for an Encounter weekend is intercession: intentional, regular, united, sober-minded intercession, and then the growing culture that follows. An Encounter is a break-through ministry, inherently surrounded by spiritual warfare. When we first started running Encounters up north, I believe our number one mistake was underestimating the significance of what we were setting out to do and the level of spiritual warfare which would accompany it. When we (Amy and my husband, Justin) were beginning our church plant, I had a difficult time believing that what I was doing was making much of a difference or was significant enough to draw fire from the enemy—was I ever wrong. I don't say this to intimidate anyone setting out to begin a new ministry. Rather, I would love to encourage you by assuring you that as you step out, even in what seem like small ways, *it really, really matters.* It is worth taking yourself and the calling the Lord has placed on your life seriously.

Before you ever place a down payment on a facility to host an Encounter, assemble a team of intercessors who will regularly pray for you, your burgeoning team, your region, and the ministry or ministries you will be interacting with. Give them a clear list of intercessory needs, including but not limited to the following concerns:

1. Protection from the plans and attacks of Satan,
2. Provision of finances, facilities and personnel,
3. Unity on your team,
4. Leadership courage, meekness, and humility, and
5. Revelation of God's heart toward you and your team throughout the process.

Once you have your intercessors in place, you can begin to address the practical details of running an Encounter Weekend. Ideally, hosting your own Encounter weekend will be the next step in the following process.

Attend an Encounter weekend, ideally with a group of key leaders, people you are relationally connected to, or just some hungry people who want more of Jesus. This is advice from Chrissy: Do it with a friend. There's nothing like the car ride home from a life-transforming event to build community, establish friendships, and continue the discipleship process.

Host or attend a Kingdom Ministry Training Site: You can begin your Encounter Builder Subscription anywhere along the way during this process; once you sign up, we will come alongside you. You can register online, and the trainings take place periodically throughout the year. See the Encounter Culture website for an up-to-date calendar of Ministry trainings and pricing. If you host as the site leader, you'll have the added advantage of being coached throughout the eight weeks, as you participate in a Kingdom Site Leader's Cohort, and have a ready pool of ministers to draw from when you're ready to staff your weekend.

The members of your Kingdom Ministry Training site do not have to have attended an Encounter Weekend, but if they would like to apprentice at an Encounter, it is essential that they attend both an Encounter Weekend as a participant and *complete Kingdom Training*. Part of the beauty of an Encounter Weekend is that those who minister have sat in the place of the participants, receiving, confessing, and experiencing the weekend from the inside. This is part of the magic sauce which makes Encounter a safe place.

Once you've *attended an Encounter* and *completed Kingdom Ministry training*, you will also personally want to *apprentice at an Encounter Weekend*. Apprenticing will allow you to taste the weekend from the "other side." You'll have the opportunity to see the inner workings of the weekend, build relationships with other hungry believers throughout your region, and pray with a wide variety of other trained prayer ministers.

***

So, to re-cap the process up to this point:

Initial Steps Before Hosting a Weekend Encounter	
1. Attend an Encounter	
2. Receive (and ideally, host as a Site Leader) Kingdom Ministry Training	
3. Participate at an Encounter Weekend as an Apprentice Prayer Minister	

Once you've checked the three boxes above, you are ready to start laying the foundation for your own weekend event. Determine who you are seeking to reach through your weekend. Are you a part of a local church, campus ministry, mom's group, fishing club, or local softball team? Having some contacts with other area ministries, churches, parachurch organizations, and schools can be helpful, but not always necessary.

At this point, we recommend beginning your *Encounter Builder Subscription Package*, and we will come alongside you throughout the process of planning, organizing, staffing, and executing your own Encounter Weekend. We look forward to coming alongside you to provide the support, experience, and resources that will help make your weekend successful. And not your weekend only: remember, the end goal in mind is cultural transformation. We want to help you assist your entire community to receive the love and freedom made available through the Cross, and then empower them to join with Jesus as He makes all things new.

Questions for prayer and reflection:

1. What is your story of Encountering God?
2. What has God set you free from?
3. Homework: Who are three friends you believe would be willing to intercede specifically and regularly for you as you lay the foundation for an Encounter in your community? Pray and reach out to them this week.
4. Make a plan to meet with your potential core team to have a "dream together" session. Write down your hopes, fears, and ideas. If this is indeed your core team, make a plan to meet together monthly for nine months, for fellowship, prayer, and practicing the 4 R's.

Notes

Notes

Financing

WE ASKED GERRY, OUR ACCOUNTING GURU, to write you a personal letter detailing how the financial breakdown of your weekend might look if you have subscribed to *Encounter Builder*. There is a blank form in the appendix for you to fill out, in order to help you create your own budget.

(We love Gerry.)

***

We are delighted that you have decided to join the Encounter family through Encounter Builder as someone who wants to run an Encounter Weekend and would like our help.

You may have noticed the subscription fee involved in running your Encounters and are concerned as to how you can afford the cost. To assist your financial concern, we have developed a financial model based on the model we use at Encounter Central, which will allow your organization to absorb the entire yearly subscription fee, as well as cover the cost of your Kingdom Ministry Training, on your first planned Encounter Weekend.

Kindly review and study the financial model with all the notes attached. We recommend that part of your weekend planning team include a person with bookkeeping/accounting experience.

Here are the steps you need to follow in order to absorb the yearly subscription fee on your first planned Encounter Weekend:

- Begin to research facilities in your area that can accommodate the size of your group. We have found that the most cost-effective facilities are retreat centers and university/college campuses.
- Contact the favored facilities to discuss housing capacity as well as dining capacity. Encounter weekends normally include two nights lodging (Friday and Saturday nights) and five meals (three Saturday, two Sunday). Obtain firm quotes from the facility, including deposit requirements and payment schedule. Request names of organizations who have previously used their facility and check their references.
- Review all the written quotes from the facilities who wish to work with you. After prayerful discernment, make a decision and contact the selected facility with a firm weekend date and deposit requirement.
- Your first Encounter Weekend should target at least 45 registrants and 15 trained prayer ministers and apprentices. Allow a few months to market your Encounter Weekends in order to reach your desired goals.

Using the above parameters, your weekend package will look as follows:

Weekend Financial Model		
Registration Income	(45 participants at $275.00/ea)	$12,375.00
Apprentice Income	(15 participants at $145.00/ea)	$2,175.00
Donations	(varies)	$500.00
Total Income		$15,050.00
Venue Expense (Lodging and Food)	(60 persons at $145.00 each)	-$8,700.00
Subscription Fee		-$2,925.00
Team Training (Kingdom Ministry Training)*		-$1,490.00
Administration Expenses		-$750.00
Total Expenses		-$13,865.00
Net Surplus		$1,185.00

* If you are running a kingdom class during your Encounter Builder subscription, the cost of the class is included.

The Weekend Financial Model reflects the costs from an actual weekend held in the northeastern United States. The key factor is to find a venue which will charge you a total of $145.00 per person to cover the room and food for the entire weekend. If your research shows that the venue expense is $20.00 more per person, then you would increase your registration fee to cover the additional expense. Likewise, if the venue cost is lower, reduce your registration fee accordingly.

If your organization requires additional assistance in developing your financial model, our Chief Financial Officer (Gerry Lachance) will gladly assist you.

Write to encounter.admin@adne.org, and use the subject: "Encounter finances with Gerry."

***

(You can see why we love Gerry.)

Questions for prayer and reflection:

1. When you think about charging for a ministry event, do you experience any "loud" thoughts or feelings? Take 15 minutes this week to "kairos" those feelings.
2. Homework: Reach out to at least three potential venues for an Encounter Weekend. With the information you receive from those venues, create a financial plan for your weekend using the appendix in the back of this manual. Send it to your intercessors for prayer.

Notes

Notes

Timelines

WE'VE BROKEN DOWN THE TIMELINE for the six months leading up to an Encounter so you can see what each person should expect to be doing when. The titles of different roles are mentioned throughout this section, such as Encounter Director, Encounter Administrator, Worship Leader, etc. The job descriptions for each of these is unpacked in Section 6, so don't despair as you look at a bunch of personnel unfamiliar to you at this point.

As far as this timeline goes, there's wiggle room. (*But for the planners among us…*)

---

9 MONTHS

☐ Encounter Director registers for Encounter Builder. This registration can pick up any time after the three steps mentioned in Section 3, "Laying the Foundations for Your Encounter Weekend." To review, these are: 1) Attend an Encounter as a participant; 2) Host a Kingdom Training Site; and 3) Attend an Encounter Weekend as an apprentice.

☐ Encounter Director begins monthly cohort coaching sessions, where he or she joins other leaders in the process of starting Encounters. During these sessions, you will have the opportunity to address each section of this manual throughout your planning process.

☐ Encounter Administrator and Encounter Director begin canvassing for the site where you'd like to hold your Encounter Weekend. It is helpful to contact a number of venues to compare prices, facilities, and available dates.

6 MONTHS

☐ Encounter Administrator finalizes dates for Encounter Weekend, reserves location, places down payment on facilities, and develops cost structure, pricing, and registration website. This information is then submitted to Encounter Culture Communications Director for the creation of a registration web page. (See the form in Appendix 2A.)

☐ Encounter Administrator develops a scholarship plan, if desired.

☐ Encounter Administrator orders promotional materials.

☐ Encounter Director reviews all session talks for the sake of familiarity, makes sure they can send them effectively to potential session teachers.

3 MONTHS

☐ Encounter Administrator updates book inventory if there will be a book table, makes sure *Kingdom Manuals* are ordered in sufficient numbers.

☐ Encounter Director chooses Prayer Ministers, Intercessors and Session Teachers, and sends session notes (see Appendix 8), slides, and session prep materials to Session Teachers.

- ☐ Worship Leader builds worship team, develops set list.

- ☐ Encounter Central launches registration, and Encounter Administrator launches registration & promotes event.

6 WEEKS

- ☐ Encounter Director checks in with Session Teachers, finishes scheduling if necessary.

- ☐ Encounter Director chooses small group leaders, room prophecy team, and A/V Leader. Fill out Encounter Team Arrival Form.

- ☐ A/V Leader contacts facility and assesses further A/V needs.

1 MONTH

- ☐ Encounter Administrator prints or sends to print shop all materials.

- ☐ Encounter Administrator plans, confirms a menu with the facility staff.

- ☐ Encounter Director meets with each Session Teacher.

- ☐ Worship Leader chooses the worship set for the weekend and forwards it to the Encounter Director for review.

- ☐ All Ministry Team should be registered by now.

2 WEEKS

- ☐ Encounter Administrator contacts facility – update about dietary restrictions

- ☐ Worship Leader sends A/V Leader worship PowerPoints

- ☐ Encounter Administrator sends PowerPoints for sessions to A/V leader

☐ Encounter Administrator completes rooming assignments for registrants to date

☐ Encounter Administrator coordinates transportation of large items (cross, fire pit)

☐ Encounter Administrator assembles "the box" (see Section 14: Materials Needed to Run your Weekend).

☐ Encounter Administrator briefs Encounter Director and any team member assigned to the welcome table on financial procedures, book sales, etc.

SUNDAY BEFORE ENCOUNTER

☐ Encounter Administrator closes registration (reserve a few extra spaces)

☐ Encounter Administrator gives final numbers to facility staff & any new dietary needs

☐ Encounter Director sends out "Encounter Week-at-a-Glance" schedule to team (see Section 12: Suggested Schedule of an Encounter Weekend)

WEEK OF ENCOUNTER

☐ Brace yourself! Remember, whatever "it" is that week, it's probably spiritual warfare.

☐ Encounter Administrator sends final email to participants, if desired

☐ Encounter Administrator prints, stuffs nametags for all registrants

☐ Encounter Administrator purchases remaining needed materials & fills Encounter boxes

☐ Encounter Administrator acquires petty cash for book sales

☐ Encounter Administrator inventories books & materials

☐ Ministry Team fasts Monday through Wednesday

☐ Ministry Team attends Pre-Encounter Prayer Meeting on Wednesday

☐ Encounter Director forms participants into small groups

ENCOUNTER FRIDAY

Suggested schedule can be edited, printed and posted in several visible locations as your team arrives.

☐ 2:00 pm – Ministry team arrives on site

☐ Check-in with retreat center staff, distribute assignments to team

☐ Set up A/V, music equipment

☐ Prepare Registration table, book table, snack table, & post signage.

☐ 3:00 pm – Room Prophecies begin

☐ 4:15 pm – Prophecies are printed, cut

☐ 4:30 pm – Ministry Team meeting begins

☐ 5:30 pm – Ministry team eats dinner together

☐ 6:00 pm – Participant Registration begins Greet participants

☐ 7:00 pm – Welcome to Encounter & housekeeping announcements

☐ Encounter begins

Homework:

1. Select dates for your Encounter Weekend.
2. Name your Administrator and Director for your weekend, share them with your intercessors.
3. Write important deadlines in your calendar. You should be working somewhere in the six month range.
4. If you are ready to select your facility, read Section 6, and then book your dates. You may need a down payment at this stage in the game. If this presents a difficulty, ask your core team if they would be willing to purchase their tickets for the weekend now, and use that income for your down payment. You'll have to do this in coordination with Encounter Central, as it will involve starting up your registration page.

Notes

Notes

Choosing Your Facility

WE'VE HELD ENCOUNTERS under some fairly interesting conditions over the years. From massive April snowstorms the day of arrival, power outages mid-PowerPoint teaching, three mid-conference sewer failures, to a six-foot abandoned pet python discovered in our dining area, having wandered in from the cold, the inconveniences and even minor crisis have become an indelible part of the story for us. Recalling the challenges we have faced is a particularly favorite pastime (not that a rogue python is a challenge, but you know...). Some of the sweetest memories include the weekends the ministry team opted to sleep on the floor to give up their beds to an overflow of participants, rather than turn them away. Many of our former participants paid it forward, covering some or all of the cost of registration so that others could experience the freedom and joy that they had tasted as a result of their weekend.

We've discovered there are a variety of creative options for Encounter venues: retreat centers and campgrounds with meeting halls and on-site catering work very well, as do some hotels with large enough conference rooms. A recent gem we've discovered is college campuses, especially in the academic off-season. *A word to the wise—I always aim for a location that is, at minimum, a 45-minute drive from the majority of any weekend's potential participants.* You don't want to choose a location so far away that it is impractical, but you also don't want to make it too convenient to drive back home. At a retreat where you examine painful aspects of your past, your relationship with God, and are surrounded by people you don't necessarily know, staying beyond Friday night can be challenging for some people, and choosing a site that is a meaningful car ride away from their house will add incentive to stick it out. It also tends to help participants prioritize the weekend, not schedule meetings, find someone else to let the dog out, etc.

Selectively choosing your facility, no matter how carefully, will never guarantee either a successful weekend or a shortage of "interesting" stories to tell future Encounter attendees, but whether you're aiming for a low-budget Encounter at an economy site or a more up-scale venue, here is a list of essentials that you'll need in whatever location you choose:

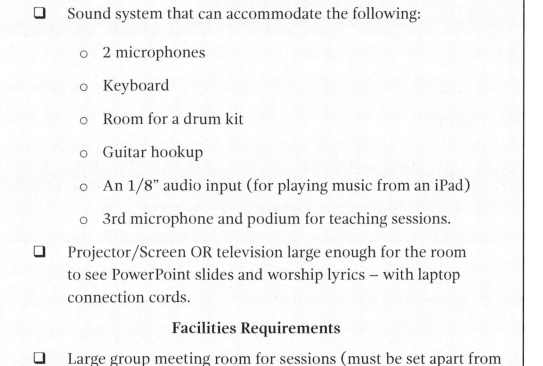

A/V Requirements

❑ Sound system that can accommodate the following:

- o 2 microphones
- o Keyboard
- o Room for a drum kit
- o Guitar hookup
- o An 1/8" audio input (for playing music from an iPad)
- o 3rd microphone and podium for teaching sessions.

❑ Projector/Screen OR television large enough for the room to see PowerPoint slides and worship lyrics – with laptop connection cords.

Facilities Requirements

❑ Large group meeting room for sessions (must be set apart from staff/other guests)

❑ Smaller meeting room for Ministry Team

❏   Suitable lodging for a minimum of 45 participants and 16 team members

❏   Printing capabilities

❏   Wireless internet (preferred)

❏   Reasonable overnight accommodations for people of varying ages/abilities. (Think of wheelchairs, mentally ill, scent allergies, CPAP machines, excessive snorers/insomniacs)

❏   Space for an outdoor campfire or campfire in a portable fire pit

❏   Food (must accommodate dietary needs of all guests), either available onsite, through a local catering service, or scheduled deliveries from a local restaurant

Homework:

Make notes about your facility of choice. Are there considerations you need to keep in mind for your target participant group, such as potential childare needs, economic stress vs. poverty mindset?

Notes

Notes

Weekend Systems Protocol

WHO DOESN'T LOVE A GOOD SYSTEM? For your weekend to have a registration website, the following steps should be followed, usually by either your Encounter Director or your State Coordinator, if you are working with one.

We have included a form for you to fill out in Appendix 2 of this manual, which will ensure you have all of your bases covered.

Step One:	Choose your dates and location and approximate the head count of your participants (how many people, including ministers, you are expecting to host for the weekend). Use our cost breakdown in Section 4 to determine the price for a participant, an apprentice prayer minister, and a full-fledged prayer minister .

Step Two:	Send this information to Encounter's Communications Director (that's us at Encounter Central), who will use it to create a registration page for your weekend on our registration platform.[1] Once you've sent your registration information to Encounter Central, our communications director will work with your Encounter Director and Administrator to determine whether you would like to sell merchandise, what kind, and potential discount codes if you will offer scholarships or discounts.
Step Three:	Your registration website should go live approximately 3 months in advance of the weekend dates. All registration and payments happen through PCO (if that is still the platform). The State Coordinators, Encounter Communication Director, and Executive Director will have access to this page, and will be able to view who has signed up and who has paid. Encounter Culture staff handles the finances for registrations and refunds. The registration page can be made available on your ministry's website if you have one, and it will also appear on the Encounter Culture website.
Step Four:	PCO automatically sends out registration confirmation emails and payment reminders until registration closes. You will have crafted your own confirmation emails and can use the appendix sample email if you'd like. Encounter Directors are listed as the primary contact for all weekend-related questions, and Encounter is to be contacted by the Encounter Director with any troubleshooting or logistical questions.

---

[1]   The major advantage to you in this is that if people are registered through our registration page, not only do you not have to manage the page, but the participants are added to our database. This means that if someone completes a Kingdom course, they can then potentially apprentice as a prayer minister at any Encounter Culture Encounter, etc.

Homework:

1. If you have not yet booked your Encounter Weekend facility, **the time is now!**
2. Submit your registration information to Encounter Central using the Systems Protocol form (see Appendix 2).
3. Check in for prayer and updates with your intercessors.
4. Read the team and job descriptions in Section 8; begin to pray and write down possible people to fill each role.
5. Review your timeline and calendar from Section 5. Finish any remaining items through six months.

Notes

Notes

Your Team for the Weekend

YOUR ENCOUNTER TEAM consists of several different roles. You will need to assemble your team and assign their roles early on in the preparation process. There are some roles that you will need to fill and some things which we at Encounter Culture will do for you—read on to find out which is which! To successfully run an Encounter Weekend, you will need:

Encounter Culture Central

Staffed by our Executive team and ministry board, we're here to help you not only run a successful Encounter Weekend but also to support you in the creation and sustaining of a culture of confession, love of Jesus, courage, and healing, that is Encounter Culture. If you are operating an Encounter Weekend through Encounter Central, all of your registrations will traffic through our system. The advantages of this are numerous: you need only to submit pre-determined information; we will craft your registration page; you have access to our database of ministers (which means you don't necessarily have to have a full team on hand, but you have the option of inviting trained ministers all over your region); everyone who attends your Encounter and a Kingdom Training Site will now be qualified to apprentice as a prayer minister at any other *Encounter Culture* Encounter.

We will also be available to you through your monthly coaching session, during which times we will progressively go over each step necessary for launching a successful Encounter Weekend. Our team is staffed by trained coaches who are eager to assist you in getting to the heart of what God is calling you to in this season, identifying what your major roadblocks are and how to overcome them, and coaching you as you work with your team as you pray, plan, and execute your Encounter Weekend. We're also there for follow up and continued equipping, resourcing, and connection as you lead into the next season.

State Coordinator

Encounter Culture (EC) works with State Coordinators to launch regional Encounters. In general, when an Encounter is launched and planned by a State Coordinator, Encounter Culture staffs the positions of Director and Administrator. If you are looking to start an Encounter, you may want to reach out to EC to see whether you have a Coordinator for your state with whom you can work to schedule and fill an Encounter. To see whether you have a State Coordinator for your state, contact Encounter Culture directly, and we'll put the two of you in touch.

State Coordinators are responsible for booking and advertising Encounter Weekends when we plan them from the center of our ministry. If you do not have a State Coordinator, or would like to work independently, the following tasks will be absorbed by your Encounter Administrator and Encounter Director:

❏ Review site requirements from the manual, select and book a site that meets the requirements for hosting an Encounter weekend

❏ If lodging is not included in your site, reach out to area hotels, hostels, university campuses, etc., to explore potential group discount rates for attendees

---

❑ Determine and submit the following information to the Encounter Communications Director for the purpose of crafting your registration web page:

» The name and contact information of venue (Comm Director will coordinate to put necessary funds down on facility), lodging possibilities for participants if separate from Encounter locale

» Cost per participant for food, lodging, and any other site-related fees

» Order promotional material from Communications Director, begin to distribute

» Determine deadline with the venue for menu and total attendance submission to venue

» Schedule promotional activities (meeting with area pastors, distributing promotional material, etc.)

» Intercede for protection, provision, and guidance

» Place down payment on facilities/meal plans

» Arrange menu and other contract details with facilities

Encounter Director

The Encounter Director oversees the recruitment, communication and pastoral care of all presenters, prayer ministry team members, and intercessors for the Encounter weekend. This is a fair-sized job which is usually filled by a *Kingdom Ministry Training Site Leader,* who has attended an Encounter Weekend, has gathered a team in the months prior, and has led them through Kingdom training (most likely, the person reading this manual), and has attended an Encounter Weekend as an Apprentice. Not everyone on your team needs to have been in your *Kingdom Site,* but it is helpful to have a relationship with some of your team members going into a weekend. If you are in need of a larger team than you can provide on your own, we can open the ministry team registration to the entire Encounter Culture community at large. This can be an exciting opportunity to work with trained ministers outside of your immediate community, reach participants who you might otherwise not have access to, and bring in apprentices from other Kingdom Training Sites. This might sound a little daunting, but the good news is that we're here to help! Remember, included with your subscription to *Encounter Builder* is ongoing coaching and resourcing as you launch your weekend.

Encounter Director Responsibilities:

- ❏ Serves as Encounter spiritual authority
- ❏ Recruits and assigns Prayer Ministers, Apprentices, session leaders, intercessors, room prophecy team, AV coordinator, and worship leader
- ❏ Plans and facilitates Mon.–Wed. prayer and fasting for Encounter and the Wednesday evening prayer and confession meeting prior to Encounter (see sample schedule, Encounter Week Schedule for Ministry Team, Section 11)
- ❏ Serves as a participant shepherd
- ❏ Oversees the pastoral care of the Ministry Team
- ❏ Selects Session teachers, provides them with session notes, PowerPoints, and "Preparing Your Testimony" notes
- ❏ Meet with each Session Teacher prior to Encounter to review testimony and talk and pray through any new conversations with God which may surface during the preparation process.
- ❏ Revises Ministry Team schedule for the weekend
- ❏ Serves as the Master of Ceremonies (may be delegated)
- ❏ Gives announcements
- ❏ Gets participants in place
- ❏ Keeps sessions and events on schedule
- ❏ Introduce speakers and sessions
- ❏ Introduces books and resources available at the book table

---

Encounter Administrator

Scope of Role:

In the past, we've had our administrator and director roles filled by two separate individuals simply because it can be a large job. I (Amy) would like you to know that it is possible to do both, but I wouldn't recommend it. Chrissy thinks it's ridiculous that I've ever done both, and she wants to assure you that it's definitely harder that way. The Encounter Administrator handles Encounter logistics, including reserving/communicating with the State Coordinator regarding the site, working with the Encounter Culture Communications Director to formulate your registration, and preparing materials. This is also the person we provide on our contact information for people who will be late to the Encounter Weekend or who have questions that they need answered either by phone or email.

Encounter Administrator Responsibilities:

❑ Works with your Encounter Director to choose dates, locate and book a facility. This can also be done in cooperation with your State Coordinator, if you have one.

❑ Communicate with the Encounter Weekend site about facility needs (A/V, etc.) & participant needs (dietary, etc.). Choose your menu, and keep track of the pricing structure.

❑ Fills out and submit to Encounter Culture all necessary information for us to create your registration web page

❑ Orders all promotional materials- available through Encounter Culture

❑ Tracks finances associated with registrations, scholarships, etc.

❑ Orders and prepare all participant materials (available through Encounter Culture)

❑ Room assignments (may delegate)

❑ Buys supplies for Encounter (see Appendix 6)

❏ Coordinates transportation for larger items (wooden cross, fire pit, etc.)
❏ Follows the protocol throughout the Encounter Weekend as detailed in the Encounter Administrator Guide (see Appendix)
❏ Answers participant questions
❏ Optional: helps coordinate transportation

Lead Intercessor

Scope of Role:

One of my favorite things about an Encounter Weekend is that it's not just the participants who receive ministry but the ministers themselves. Our Lead Intercessor is a person on the ministry team designated to receive what the team feels God may be saying about the weekend and communicate that to the Director, intercede throughout the weekend, receive and give feedback from and to the Encounter Director, and also offer prayer ministry to any ministers who need it.

Lead Intercessor Responsibilities:

❏ Collects passages of scripture, dreams, and impressions from the team regarding upcoming Encounters and makes them available to the Encounter Director; some directors may like to have these shared at the mandatory Ministry Team Prayer Meeting, which occurs the Wednesday night prior to your Encounter Weekend.
❏ Intercedes before, during, and after Encounter Weekend
❏ Provides intercession and prayer ministry support to the ministry team throughout Encounter Weekend.
❏ Ministers to participants, if desired by Director
❏ Prays over the facility, including all meeting rooms and bedrooms, etc.

- ❑ Intercedes for participants as spiritual warfare becomes evident
- ❑ Stays aware of the needs of the room, supplying blessed elements, and other support as needed.

Worship Leader

Scope of Role:

In communication with the Encounter Director, prepare and lead worship appropriate for each session.

Worship Leader Responsibilities:

- ❑ Prepares worship sets for each worship session throughout the Encounter Weekend.
- ❑ Submits worship plan to the Ministry Team Leader one month prior to Encounter
- ❑ Prepare PowerPoint with the lyrics: Send a copy to the A/V Coordinator and Ministry Team Leader at least 2 weeks prior to the event. Bring a copy on a flash drive to the event.
- ❑ Arrive early enough to set up instrument(s) and do a sound check prior to Encounter Leaders prayer meeting
- ❑ Print and bring copies of all music for each musician
- ❑ Coordinate with A/V Coordinator to gather all equipment necessary for worship (i.e., cords, stands, mics, monitors, etc.)

A/V Leader

Scope of Role:

Oversees all media preparations and implementation for the Encounter weekend. Most seasoned AV leaders I know would appreciate the brevity of this narrative section—so let's get to the point!

Worship Leader Responsibilities:

- ❑ Creates a worshipful and aesthetically pleasing environment
- ❑ Works with Worship Leader and Encounter Director for cues in worship and ministry
- ❑ Works with Session Teachers to make sure PPTs are set for session talks
- ❑ Becomes familiar with equipment and programs at the facility prior to Encounter Weekend
- ❑ Assesses A/V needs above & beyond what is at the facility
- ❑ Transports equipment
- ❑ Sets up equipment
- ❑ Runs PPT during Encounter
- ❑ Provides PPT and music transitions between and during sessions
- ❑ DJs music—suggested set lists available upon request
- ❑ Runs soundboard

Prayer Ministers

Scope of Role:

Be present to God, the Ministry Team, and to the participants as you minister to the people at Encounter God weekend. A minister must have completed the eight-week Kingdom Ministry Training course, attended an Encounter as a participant, and then as an apprentice.

Prayer Minister Responsibilities:

- ❑ To participate in all Ministry Team prayer meetings & fast before the weekend
- ❑ To live a lifestyle in accordance with Encounter Culture (i.e., confessional, in community with other believers, pursuing holiness of life and love of God and neighbor)

❑ To help facilitate an environment of safety and hospitality for the participants

❑ To abide by the Prayer Minister contract, including maintaining confidentiality

❑ To participate in all Ministry Team meetings before, during, and after the Encounter Weekend

❑ To listen to God and participants, ask for appropriate permissions (ex., "May I place a hand on your shoulder while I pray for you?"), and pray for the participants during ministry time and as requested

❑ To serve on the Room Prophesy Team and/or small groups, as invited

Session Teachers

Scope of Role:

Session Teachers are Prayer Ministers who have the added responsibility of presenting a teaching session and sharing their testimony. The scope of their role includes teaching from the Encounter Curriculum as presented in session notes under the oversight of the Encounter Director and providing testimony that enriches the session talk. It is a challenging, sometimes exciting, and sometimes daunting thing to engage the process of moving our stories of healing into actual testimony. To name our own sins and testify to the greatness of God toward us can be a powerful part of our own journey toward healing and victory.

In the weeks leading up to an Encounter, I (Amy) make sure to meet with each minister who is presenting a session, to pray with them, help them to process and pray through their written testimony, and encourage them as they prepare. I often invite Apprentice Prayer ministers to serve in this role if I feel that it would benefit and not overwhelm them. The benefits of sharing your story of redemption are immense: keep in mind, however, that though all of our stories are ongoing, and oftentimes healing is a process, *testimony* needs to be sourced from a realm of some breakthrough or healing, not simply an area where you are aware of pain or sin.

Session Teacher Responsibilities:

❏ To study and prepare for the talk 4–6 weeks before the Encounter Weekend

❏ To write out a testimony that gives the session some depth and increases faith, following the "Preparing Your Testimony" guidelines outlined in the Appendix of this manual (see Appendix 3: Sample Testimony Preparation Letter)

❏ To meet with the Encounter Director before the Weekend to review testimony and receive prayer.

❏ To participate in all Ministry Team prayer meetings & fasting days before the weekend

---

Apprentices

Scope of Role:

An Apprentice fills a dual role of learner and minister. Apprentices are present throughout the preparation and execution of an Encounter Weekend, but in order to cultivate confidence and skill, they are always paired with a diversity of seasoned Prayer Ministers. It is important that Apprentices are paired with different Prayer Ministers throughout an Encounter Weekend in order to expose them to a variety of different personalities, giftings, and styles of healing prayer. It is to the great advantage of any growing ministry team that new ministers are not formed as replicas of one individual but rather are exposed to great diversity within the realm of good practice and given the space to become the ministers God is calling them to be. When leading an Encounter, I (Amy) make a point of checking in with our Apprentices regularly throughout the weekend and also encouraging whichever Prayer Ministers I have partnered them with for each session to take time to debrief with them as well. Before stepping into the role of Apprentice, one must have attended the eight-week Kingdom Ministry Training course and have attended an Encounter Weekend as a participant.

Apprentice Responsibilities:

❑ To learn, observe, and grow as a prayer minister
❑ To take every advantage of the opportunity to engage the challenges which arise throughout the preparation process and the Encounter Weekend itself.
❑ Same as Prayer Ministers, but always in conjunction with seasoned Prayer Ministers, not with other Apprentices or alone.

***

Questions for reflection:

1. Ministering with Apprentices is one of the ways we form a culture which continues to reproduce itself rather than just create professionals in the center. But bringing in new people can be a messy process, especially if they're not very far along on their own journey of healing themselves. What are your hopes and fears in regards to taking on apprentices? What are you most committed to reproducing? What makes a good apprentice?
2. What does your heart have to say about leadership in the Kingdom of God? What does your head say?

Homework:

1. Solidify your team using the jobs and job descriptions in this chapter. Now is a good time to start your "blue binder" (see Appendix 7, beginning with Form 7B, "Ministry Team Assignments").

2. If you have not yet gathered your ministry team in full, this is the time to do it. Review all session notes for your upcoming Encounter ("Come Like Peter," "Sin," "The Cross," etc.), and prayerfully assign each session to one of your Prayer Ministers or Apprentices. Read Section 9 when you've confirmed each session, and send your presenters the materials as listed in Section 9, Teaching and Testimony (notes, PowerPoints, etc.).

3. Using your new registration page, you should now begin marketing for your upcoming Encounter Weekend.

Notes

Notes

SECTION 9

Teaching and Testimony

ONE OF MY (AMY'S) FAVORITE ASPECTS of running an Encounter is preparing Session Teachers to present and give their testimony. I love the liminal space of someone's story of pain becoming their story of healing and freedom, and then seeing the releasing of that story set other people free. The Encounter Director prayerfully invites each presenter to give one of the eight sessions. You can look over the sessions (Come Like Peter, Sin, the Cross, Healing our Image of God, Sexual Wholeness, Keys to the Kingdom, Be Filled, and Run with the Vision) in Part III, "Session Notes." When Session Teachers agree to share their stories, the Encounter Director needs to send each presenter the following:

- notes for their session (see Part III),
- the PowerPoint presentation slides for their session, and
- an email detailing what is expected of them as a presenter and some guidelines for preparing their testimony.

I arrange a meeting with each presenter prior to the Encounter to pray with them. We go over what they will share, and I offer any helpful counsel or encouragement. I also instruct them that once they have met with me, they are not to change anything. The temptation to second-guess one's presentation at the last minute is very high, so I make sure to let the presenters know about this potential pitfall and encourage them to share at the Encounter what they have already shared with me.

We always emphasize that presenters are to teach the session notes *exactly* as they are written, with no exceptions, without prior approval and from the Encounter Director. We do this for three primary reasons:

1. The experience of confessing our sin and bondage and then turning it into a testimony to set others free is a powerful step in healing. It is a great delight not only to be set free but then to return to the site of the prison and plunder the enemy's camp, releasing others as well. For this to be possible for everyone— not just the confident and engaging public speakers among us—it is important to have solid teachings everyone can access.

2. Having pre-written teachings ensures theological orthodoxy and continuity throughout the weekend. It enables everyone (not just those with a seminary degree) to "play" while maintaining the integrity of the teachings.

3. An Encounter Weekend is a delicate balance as far as time is concerned. If Session Teachers consistently go off script, the potential for running out of time for ministry is very high.

Releasing the Power of Your Testimony

When we prepare speakers to present their session, the possibilities—what to say, how much to share, how much time they can take—can be overwhelming. As a result, I send clear guidelines for testimony preparation. There is some variation for each presenter, depending on which session they are giving (for example, whoever gives the talk on the Holy Spirit generally testifies about their experience with the Holy Spirit, and whoever presents on Healing Our Image of God generally shares a way in which their image of God was broken and has been healed, etc.). I have each presenter answer the following questions and use the answers as the outline for their testimony.

1. What have you been set free from? *Name the sin.*

2. How did the sin impact your life? Relationships? Prayer? *Be specific.*

3. Who was hurt by your sin? *What happened?*

4. How did you come to realize it was sin?

5. What did God do for you? *How are you changed?*

> *Now unto him that is able to keep you from falling, and to present you faultless before the presence of his glory with exceeding joy, To the only wise God our Saviour, be glory and majesty, dominion and power, both now and ever. Amen.*
>
> *Jude 1:24–25*

Sometimes it can feel tricky to share stories involving people (such as parents) who are still alive in a way that is honest but not slanderous toward them. Therefore, I include the following coaching notes in the preparation email that I send out. In addition, I usually anticipate a conversation about any sticky bits when we get together to pray before they present.

- All people (including parents) are broken. All parents wound their children.

- Hopefully, one day your children, should you have them, will be testifying of their own freedom from parental wounds.

- Own all personal sin. There are three tendencies when dealing with parental wounds: the first is denial (particularly in Christian communities); the second is laying the blame for personal sin on parents (acting the permanent victim, psychologizing sin); and the third is minimizing the pain, and skipping right to forgiveness from the vantage point of your adult analysis of the situation.

Basic Guidelines for Presentations

Each session in its entirety (notes and slides along with the testimony) must be limited to no more than **30 minutes**; this will leave ample time for ministry.

That said, no matter how much time is spent on preparation, an Encounter Weekend is a bit of a live animal and can be somewhat unpredictable, particularly where the sessions are concerned. Your presenters are human and, importantly, mostly non-professional public speakers (or even more likely to go long on time—pastors!). Any time you hand over the microphone, there is a margin of—let us say—*possibility*. Do the best you can to prepare, but also know that it is possible to make a little margin throughout the weekend by moving small group meetings to mealtimes if needed. If your speaker is going way over time, take a deep breath and assess the situation. Is the Lord at work in a way that you just want to make more room for? If, for example, the Lord is moving on a presenter and the expression of emotions (tears, etc.) makes the session go a bit long, don't sweat it! But do avoid the mentality that it is always the Lord if anybody goes off script or takes 60 minutes instead of their prescribed 30. Plan a polite signal, and tell your team that you will signal to them if they're going too long. Again, before you use your signal, weigh the cost-benefit ratio: is what is happening right now productive, or has someone gone off script and is now just storytelling? Are they going so much over time that you're going to miss lunch, or can you budget ten or fifteen minutes from small group sessions later in the day?

I have come to enjoy the live unpredictability of welcoming the non-A-team to share their stories and present sessions. There is something incredibly powerful about having the space to be an imperfect human. If participants see imperfect humans sharing their stories, they may not be as entertained as they would be if every session were flawless and given by professionals. Still, they may actually be able to see themselves in the presenters, and also *as* the presenters. Remember, your hope is that participants will someday soon become ministers themselves. If the bar for a successful presentation is too high, you'll scare off most everyday people who fear public speaking more than death itself! Do your best to manage what can be managed, and learn to trust God with the vulnerable, messy spaces that you cannot control.

Homework:

1. Review one of your own stories about Encounter with God. If possible, try to make this story one that is fresh—something you have been recently set free from or a way in which God has recently transformed you. Remember, a testimony is a story that is at least partially in the history department—you've received some level of freedom or healing. This shouldn't be a completely "cliff-hanger" story, but one which includes breakthrough, even if the story continues. If it is helpful to you, you can utilize your answers from earlier on in Encounter Builder, your testimony (if you've given one) from a past Encounter, or the work that you did during Kingdom Site Leader coaching. Decide which session you would like to teach at your upcoming Encounter.

2. Send notes and slides to each presenter, along with an email with instructions for preparing their testimony. Work with each session leader to put a meeting time with you on the calendar sometime within the two or three weeks leading up to your Encounter Weekend.

Notes

Notes

Ministry Assignments
for the Weekend

Small Group Leaders

Scope of Role:

To create a space where external processors can explore what God is speaking to them and what they are going to do about it; to demonstrate love and active listening; to provide intercessors with insight into how best to pray.

Responsibilities:

- ❑ Create an environment of belonging and of a shared journey.
- ❑ Ask the provided small group questions at the appropriate time.
- ❑ Demonstrate active listening, compassion, and gentleness.
- ❑ Facilitate conversation in a respectful and time-sensitive manner so everyone has a chance to share, without any one person being forced to share.
- ❑ Listen to the Holy Spirit and their heart behind their answer.

❏ Be aware of your own reactions, judgments, and motives.
❏ Affirm each participant and model safe and healthy interaction.
❏ Occasionally share if there is a general mood, apathy, or resistance to the Holy Spirit to the Ministry Team Leader and the Intercessors after the small group meets. Share if that changes throughout the weekend.
❏ Do not teach; you may clarify if it's needed for someone to feel loved and included.

Welcome Table Staff

Scope of Role:

To manage registration and the sale of resources in a manner consistent with the Encounter Weekend.

Responsibilities:

❏ Organize welcome table with nametags, necessary forms, participant handbooks, spiritual profiles, and other resources (books, t-shirts, etc.).
❏ Exercise responsibility over books, cash box, credit card technology, tablecloth and suggested donation lists.
❏ Be somewhat familiar with the resources available in order to answer basic questions.
❏ Record sales in accordance with Director and Administrator policy.
❏ Responsible for set up and take down of table.

Room Prophecy Team

Room prophecies are a fascinating and exciting part of an Encounter Weekend. Before anybody other than possibly the Encounter Administrator knows what rooms each person (team included) will be staying in, the Room Prophecy team takes a tour of the venue and prays over each room. Designate one person on the team to take notes while the group listens to the Lord for words of knowledge and encouragement for the people who will be staying in each room. Room prophecies should align with our "Prophetiquette for Encounter Weekend Room Prophecies" guidelines, which should be reviewed by the Director and Room Prophecy team before setting out on their prayer tour. Also helpful here may be a glance at Appendix D on page 86 of the Kingdom Ministry Training Manual.

Prophetiquette for Encounter Weekend Room Prophecies:

❑ No "dates, mates, or babies."
❑ Avoid terms or phrases which are not readily understood by everybody, Christians or otherwise.
❑ Listen for the heart of God, scripture passages, words of encouragement, identity, and freedom that God has in store.

***

Example of a Ministry Team Assignment Worksheet

Name	Session	Function	Set Up
1. Abraham Rogers	Come Like Peter	Prayer Minister	Snack Table
2. Sarah Smith	Sin	Apprentice	Room Prophecy Team 1
3. Jacob Redford	The Cross	Prayer Minister	Room Prophecy Team 1 Leader
4. Isaac Washington	Healing Our Image of God	Prayer Minister	Room Prophecy Team 1
5. David Goldsmith	Sexual Wholeness Men	Worship Leader, Prayer Minister	AV Leader
6. Rebecca Doorman	Sexual Wholeness Women	Director, Prayer Minister	Welcome Table, Director
7. Leah Baker	Keys of the Kingdom	Apprentice	Welcome Table
8. Samuel Hornblower	Be Filled	Prayer Minister	Room Prophecy Team 2
9. Saul Markson	Run With the Vision	Prayer Minister	Room Prophecy Team 1 Leader
10. Abigail Peterson		Administrator, Prayer Minister	Welcome Table, Registration
11. Mary LeBlanc		Apprentice	Room Prophecy 2
12. Peter Lee		Apprentice	Room Prophecy 2
13. John Bennett		Prayer Minister	Registration, Signage
14. Mark Stone		Prayer Minister, AV	Room Prophecy Team 1
15. Sampson Chin		Prayer Minister	Chair Set Up
16. Paul Akinyemi		Apprentice	Snack Table
17. Jorham McPhearson		Prayer Minister	Welcome Table, Registration
18.			

19.			
20.			
21.			
22.			

Homework:

1. Begin to fill out your ministry assignments form (see Appendix 7B). This will be an ongoing task, as you may not have completely solidified your ministry/apprentice team for the weekend.
2. Re-read Appendix D on page 86 of the *Kingdom Ministry Training Manual.* Come prepared to your next cohort for a conversation about prophetic ministry, safe culture, and growing up in love.

Notes

Notes

Encounter Week Schedule for Ministry Team

I (Amy) always send the following schedule out in an email to everyone on the team the Sunday night before Encounter. I include a Zoom link for our Wednesday night prayer meeting if we are meeting online rather than in person and a brief word about fasting. If you will be having a formal debriefing session, let them know when and where in this email as well (see Appendix 7I, "Debrief Report"). Sometimes in lieu of a formal debriefing session, I may take the team out for appetizers following Sunday clean-up, and we celebrate and debrief then.

This email is also a great opportunity to share a word of encouragement or what you have been hearing from the Lord as you have been praying for your team.

***

Monday-Wednesday, May 11-13

- Personal fasting and prayer for participants and the weekend.
- Make sure to record any scripture or prophetic impressions you may receive and bring them to the prayer meeting.

Wednesday, May 13

| 6:30 pm | Prayer meeting (provide Zoom link and/or physical address) |

Friday, May 15: Encounter Weekend!

2:30 pm	Arrival/setup/prayer over the building.
3:00 pm	Small group informational meeting. You will meet with the Small Group Leader for training if you are leading or helping in a small group. If you are not involved in this, you will be continuing with A/V or registration setup, etc.
3:30 pm	Ministry Team will begin praying over rooms.
4:30 pm	All Encounter Ministry Team prayer and briefing. All team members must be on time for this meeting. See Ministry Team Director for meeting location.
5:30 pm	Enjoy dinner together. Bring your own food and eat in the dining room.
6:00 pm	Be ready to welcome participants and make them feel comfortable.
7:00 pm	Encounter Begins!

Questions for prayer and discussion:

1. What has God been saying to you throughout this process of planning, learning, and interacting with your team?

2. Where do you see God at work in your team as you prepare for your Weekend? Are there unexpected blessings, or challenges, that have arisen?

3. What is your plan for personal confession leading up to Encounter? How are you being intentional about not "flying with 'bombs' in your luggage"?

Notes

Notes

Fasting,
Encounter Week Prayer Meeting,
and the Afterparty

IN THE WEEK LEADING UP to each Encounter Weekend, we require all of our team to take part in three days of fasting and prayer and attend a mandatory group prayer and worship meeting on the Wednesday night prior to the start of Encounter.

Why Fast?

We fast prior to an Encounter Weekend for several reasons. We fast because it reflects, in a small way, what is actually true. When we experience and embrace our weakness (the weakness we feel in our bodies when we fast), we connect in a deeper way to the reality that what really sustains us: the power to transform lives, heal bodies, and set people free, all comes from God. It's easy to go about our lives feeling self-sufficient most of the time and to minister out of our own strength and what we think is possible within the scope of that strength. Fasting reminds us that we need more than we currently have and that we long for God to enter into our weakness and the pain and brokenness we will see before us at an Encounter. Fasting is an expression of our longing for more of God, His presence, power, and love. As such, it is also an act of spiritual warfare. We are inviting and asking God to come and do what only He can do: set the captive free, give sight to the blind, and heal the brokenhearted.

Fasting is a new experience for many Encounter Prayer Ministers, so I will often write a short blurb along with my Encounter Week Schedule email inviting them to learn a little more about fasting, explaining the kind of fasts that we can engage in, such as individual meals, solid food, all food, or certain types of foods, and for those of us for whom food fasting is medically unadvisable, fasts of other kinds such as radical financial giving, abstaining from media to make increased time and mental/emotional clarity for intercession, etc.

One of the best and most accessible resources I have found on the heart and practice of fasting is the article "Your Personal Guide to Fasting and Prayer" by Dr. Bill Bright, founder of Campus Crusade and consummate practitioner of fasting and prayer.[1] I recommend reading it.

When an Encounter has been completed, it is also important to make intentional time for debriefing your team and celebrating what the Lord has done. People who have been on the front lines together need to share their stories, air questions or struggles that may have arisen and give thanks to God for all He has done in and through them. Unless you're a real party animal, making time for celebration can be one of the more challenging aspects of Encounter planning. So if you need a bit of a case built as you make your plans, consider the following reasons.

Why Celebrate?

First and foremost, we celebrate because our God is primarily a happy God. Hebrews Chapter 1, speaking of Jesus, states: "Your throne, O God, will last for ever and ever; a scepter of justice will be the scepter of your kingdom. You have loved righteousness and hated wickedness; therefore *God, your God, has set you above your companions by anointing you with the oil of joy*" (italics mine). Jesus is actually the happiest person alive, so we embrace joyful celebration in response to and in agreement with His joy.

Practically speaking, we celebrate because we feed what we want to see grow. If we want to develop a joyful, confident community that loves Jesus,

---

[1] Article is available here: https://www.cru.org/us/en/train-and-grow/spiritual-growth/fasting/personal-guide-to-fasting.html

lives vulnerably, and prays for others, we need to see each time this happens as a "win" and take the time to bless it and celebrate it.

Celebration is, in part, an act of thanksgiving (1 Thessalonians 5:18)—turning and offering back to God that which He has given and done, or closing the relational circuit, if you will.

Resistance to Celebration and Leading Others into Celebration:

1. Not receiving the "Good job" from the Father ourselves due to having a slave/orphan heart rather than the heart of a son
2. Having a critical spirit: "It's never good enough"
3. Being too busy to slow down; feeling like celebration is a waste of time
4. Misplaced "wins"—only celebrating the "big" things (i.e., major healing or breakthrough, etc.)

Questions to Provoke Celebration, Thanksgiving, and Growth:

These are available to copy in Appendix 7H.

1. What did I enjoy most about this journey?
2. What did I do well?
3. What strengths did I use?
4. What skills did I gain?
5. What do I feel most confident about?
6. Were there obstacles that I overcame? How did I do it?
7. Where was God in this for me?

***

Questions for prayer and discussion:

1. How do I feel about celebrating a ministry event?
2. What would measurable success look like for this Encounter?

Homework:

1. Review the Debrief Report for Encounter Weekend (Appendix 71). Circulate it amongst your team leaders, so they can come prepared to debrief your Encounter when the time comes.
2. Schedule a debrief and celebration meeting with your Encounter team.
3. Send out an email to your team regarding fasting, fasting dates, and your pre-Encounter prayer meeting.
4. Assign the job of planning the "afterparty" to a member of your team. This gathering can be as simple as stopping at a restaurant as a team on the way home from your Encounter, or it can be an event that requires more planning. The party planner needs to know that they are in charge of communicating the date and location of the debrief/party to each team member.

Notes

Notes

Suggested Schedule of an Encounter Weekend

CREATE A SCHEDULE THAT WORKS with the venue you have chosen. The major variable tends to be mealtimes: some places have specific, set mealtimes, and some have a fair amount of flexibility. Also, you'll see several openings for small group times—the only one of these I *always* keep is the first one on Friday night, when we introduce the participants to their small group leader(s). After that, I use the small group time as a flex time, making space in the weekend if ministry times go particularly long. If I scrap the Saturday small group meetings, I usually have the groups sit together for meals other than breakfasts (who wants a small group meeting at breakfast?!), which has worked well for us over the years.

The schedule which follows can be modified, put in your program, and posted on walls/doors throughout your meeting facility.

***

FRIDAY	*Come Ready*
4:30 pm	Leadership Team Prayer
6:00	Registration
8:30	Ministry Time
7:00	Welcome & Orientation
7:15	Worship
7:45	Come Like Peter
9:00	Small Group Time
9:30	Fellowship Time
11:00	Quiet/Lights Out

SATURDAY	*Discover the Heart of God*
7:15 am	Leadership Team Prayer
8:00	Breakfast
9:00	Worship
9:15	Sin: The Way of Death
9:40	Break
10:00	The Cross
10:25	Ministry Time
11:45	Lunch
12:30 pm	Break/Leadership Prayer
1:00	Worship
1:15	Healing our Image of God
1:40	Ministry Time/Break
3:00	Sexual Wholeness
3:30	Ministry Time
4:30	Small Groups
5:00	Dinner/Break
5:40	Leadership Prayer
6:00	Worship
6:30	Closing Doors
7:15	Ministry Time
9:00	Testimonies, Fire, and/or Dance party
11:00	Quiet/Lights Out

SUNDAY	*Leave Changed!*
7:30 am	Leadership Team Prayer
8:00	Breakfast
9:00	Worship
10:45	Run with the Vision
9:30	Igniting the Fire
9:55	Ministry Time
11:25	Testify
12:00 pm	Lunch
1:00	Leave Changed!

Notes

Notes

Materials Needed to Run Your Weekend

HERE'S A LIST OF SUPPLIES that you'll need for each Encounter. There's a checklist in the appendix which can be copied, and—just a hint—we laminate the checklist and adhere it to the boxes where we keep all our Encounter materials. That way, when it comes time to run a weekend, we can quickly inventory the boxes and fill them according to the checklist on the box.

Also, a word about the infamous "blue binder," which is the binder we assemble and take to each Encounter that holds all of our printed materials, checklists, session notes, and weekend team assignments: It doesn't have to be blue. Ours just is.

- ❏ Pens—60
- ❏ Tissues—6 boxes (2 for front, 1 for each corner of room)
- ❏ Mints
- ❏ Permanent markers
- ❏ Tape and/or poster gum
- ❏ 2 tablecloths (logo tablecloths optional)
- ❏ Signage (posted weekend schedule, welcome banner optional)

- ❐ Square reader, or other credit card reader, with accompanying device and appropriate app.

- ❐ Earplugs

- ❐ Name tag lanyards

- ❐ Laptop for registrations

- ❐ Laptop for PowerPoints throughout weekend

- ❐ Laptop for room prophecies

- ❐ Kingdom Manuals, Encounter promotional materials

- ❐ "The Blue Binder," which includes:

    - ❑ Encounter Director handbook

    - ❑ Enough laminated copies of "Prayers of Protection" and "Cutting Free" for the ministry team

    - ❑ Laminated notes for each teaching presentation for the person who will be running PowerPoint, and an extra copy for each session presenter

    - ❑ Registration check-in

    - ❑ Sales forms

    - ❑ Small group list

    - ❑ A map of the facility if available

    - ❑ Ministry Team Set-up form

    - ❑ Encounter Administrator Weekend Guide

    - ❑ Any additional prayer liturgies (breaking soul-ties, identificational prayers of repentance for mothers and fathers, etc.), laminated

- ❐ Spiritual profiles

- ❐ Participant Handbooks

- ❐ Holy Water

- ❐ Blessed Oil & Salt

- ❏ Extra Prayer liturgies
- ❏ Passion DVD or digital copy
- ❏ Cash box with cash
- ❏ New Names
- ❏ Other Supplies
- ❏ Cross
- ❏ Nails
- ❏ Hammers
- ❏ Fire pit
- ❏ Logs
- ❏ Kindling
- ❏ Newspaper
- ❏ Lighter
- ❏ Price lists

See Appendix 6 for checklist.

Notes

Notes

Registration, Websites, and Liability Waivers

THE FOLLOWING PAGES ARE AN OVERVIEW of what we will contribute to your registration webpage in regard to information collected and the liability waiver, which we require all participants and ministers to sign. If you have questions or would like to propose changes to your registration page, please contact our communications director.

Registration

The following information is a sample of what will be collected from registrants when they sign up for an Encounter Weekend. All information is confidential and not shared with anyone outside our organization.

Name, First & Last	
Email Address	
Home Address	

Phone Number	
Emergency Contact	
Birthday*	
Church Name (if any)	
How did you hear about the Encounter God Weekend?	(multiple choice)
Emergency Contact: Name, Relation, Phone Number	
Do you have any allergies or dietary restrictions?	
Are there any health concerns you would like the Ministry Team to be aware of?	
Do you have any other special needs or requirements?	
Would you like to receive our monthly newsletter?	
Do you plan on bringing an infant? We would love to help accommodate children under one year of age.**	

*If there are minors at any event, we require a separate permission form to be signed by a parent or guardian and submitted at check-in.

**Some facilities require that infants in attendance be registered, and some do not. We register all infants and charge a nominal fee to help cover the cost of childcare during ministry sessions. We require that infants be registered at least two weeks prior to the event to give us the necessary time to hire screened and vetted childcare. All of our hired childcare must be in compliance with our current diocesan safe childcare standards. For more information, please go to adne.org/resources.

Liability Waiver *(sample text)*

1. I wish to participate in the Encounter Weekend (Event). I understand that my execution of this Waiver and Release is a prerequisite for participation in the Event. I further understand that there are risks and dangers inherent in participating in this Event.

2. I understand that in order to be allowed to participate in the Event, I agree to assume all risks and to release and hold harmless (Sponsoring church or ministry), Encounter Culture, the Anglican Diocese in New England (ADNE), Anglican Church in North America (ACNA), (The Retreat Center or Facility), and their officers, agents, employees, assigns, successors in interest, contractors, vendors (and their agents), agencies, sponsors, officials and volunteers, including host families, grounds facilitators, participating communities and organizations and all governmental and public entities including, but not limited to, the State, County and local municipalities where the Event takes place (collectively the "Released Parties").

3. I intend by this Waiver and Release to release, in advance, and to waive my rights and to indemnify, defend, and hold harmless the Released Parties with respect to any cost, expense, liability or damage, including reasonable attorneys' fees and expenses related to the investigation or defense of any claims (collectively, "Damages") incurred if and to the extent that such Damages result from claims resulting from the activities or on account of any actions, negligent or otherwise, of the Released Parties. I understand and agree that this Waiver and Release is binding on my heirs, assigns, and legal representatives.

4. I understand that I am solely responsible for adequate personal property and liability insurance to cover any and all contingencies during the entire duration of the Event, including all travel time.

5. I understand that I am solely responsible for my health and safety, and I acknowledge that I am physically capable of participating in and completing this Event.

6. Should any portion of this Waiver and Release be judicially determined invalid, voidable, or unenforceable for any reason, such portion of this Waiver and Release shall be severable from the remaining portions herein and the invalidity, voidability, or unenforceability thereof shall not affect the validity, effect, enforceability, or interpretation of the remaining provisions of this Waiver and Release.

7. I have carefully read this Waiver and Release and fully understand its contents. If under the age of eighteen, my parent or legal guardian has completely reviewed this Waiver and Release, understands and consents to its terms, and authorizes my participation by checking the agreement box below. I understand that this is a legally binding digital signature. I am aware that this is a RELEASE OF LIABILITY and a contract between me and the persons and entities mentioned above, and I sign of my own free will.

Notes

Notes

SECTION 16

Style Guidelines,
Brand Kit Access

FROM ANCIENT EGYPTIAN HIEROGLYPHIC BRANDS denoting cattle ownership, to the pictorial signs over pubs and blacksmiths of the Middle Ages, to our modern industry of logo creation and brand design, crafting symbols help those outside of our ministries, companies, and organizations both understand and recognize who we are and what we do. At Encounter Culture, we have two images that we incorporate into all our materials and taglines. These help orient those who engage our ministries as to who we are and what they can expect from us as far as ministry, ministry practices, and theological framework. If you are planning an Encounter Culture event (and if you've gotten this far in the manual, we'll assume you're at least interested), we require our brand kit to be the one you use on your advertisements, programs, websites, etc. Of course, you are very welcome to branch out on your own at any time, and we always thank God for more laborers in the fields, whether or not they are working specifically with us on the ground. If you plan to run an Encounter Weekend through the Encounter Culture ministry and have purchased a subscription to Encounter Builder, you will receive a zip file that includes access to our brand kit, color palette numbers, tagline (come ready, leave changed), and our fonts.

A word about our logos:

We have chosen a keyhole to represent Encounter Culture. The keyhole symbolizes our fervor for seeing people set free from bondage and pain

through the ministry of Jesus at the cross and the power of the Holy Spirit. It also shows our passion for equipping the whole body to have access to unlock that same freedom and share it with others. I love the logo because it reminds me that there are no doors that Jesus doesn't have the keys to unlock: there is nothing too broken to fix or so hidden that He cannot find it. So often, the enemy tells us that our pain is too endlessly complicated, too big, or too unique for the cross to actually matter to us. But the reality is that's just not true. At Encounter Culture, we love listening to others, helping them find the door that the pain or sin or trauma is hiding behind, and together asking Jesus to come and unlock that door, turn the lights on, clean out the garbage, and fill the room with promise, identity and presence.

On all Encounter Weekend programs and t-shirts, you'll see the image of

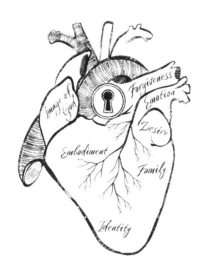

the human heart with a keyhole in the upper middle. I am regularly informed by well-meaning people that the image of a human heart is grotesque for a ministry logo, that the image is jarring and maybe a little ugly. And to this I say: *Exactly.* An Encounter Weekend isn't pretty: an encounter with the living God means the things deep inside of us (such as pain that feels so normal that we can think it *is* us) are brought into the light of His truth, His cross, and His healing. When we encounter God, we start to see things as they actually are. As our eyes are opened, and we say out loud the things which have kept us bound, many things that are just as hidden to the naked eye as the human heart from the outside of a human body are made visible. Our humanity, our human-ness, can be a hard to look at: we prefer to present things in a tidy, socially acceptable, or even impressive way. An Encounter Weekend is an opportunity to bring our hearts out where they can be seen and healed.

Notes

PART II

Appendices

Financing Your Encounter Weekend Worksheet

Expenses	Price per person	Total cost
*Venue (room & board, expense per participant)		
*Subscription Fee		
Kingdom Ministry Training		
Administration Expenses		
Total Expense:		
Income		
Participant Registration Fee		
**Apprentice Registration Fee		
***Prayer Minister Registration Fee		
Donations		
Total Income:		

*Combine these two numbers to get the price per participant. This information will be used to create your registration fee. Caclulate the registration fee based on a minimum of 45 participants in order to cover cost.

**We charge our apprentices venue costs + administration fee + $40.

***We charge our prayer ministers venue costs + administration fee

111

APPENDIX 2A

Systems Protocol Form

Encounter Weekend Systems Form:

Please complete and return to Encounter Culture a minimum of four months prior to your scheduled Encounter Weekend.

Event Title	Encounter Weekend; If you have a subcategory, list here (i.e. pastors and ministry leaders, women, etc.):
State Coordinator/Director	
Venue/Location	
Start Date & Time	End Date & Time
Additional Information	

Checklist	Response
Venue Cost per person (*if lodging is separate, see below)	
Estimated # of Participants	
By what date is a downpayment required by venue	
Deadline for menu submission	
What is the venue deadline for submission of total registrants	
Amt. promotional material needed	
*off-site lodging needed? List venues, cost	

Event Categories: Optional section

Additional Notes	Category	Type	Assigned to	Totals

Key Contacts for the Event:

Name	Phone #	Email Address	Website	Name	Phone #	Email Address	Website
State Coordinator							
Encounter Director							
Venue Contact							
Encounter Culture		encounterculture.admin@adne.org					
*off-site caterer							
*off-site lodging							

Sample Welcome Email for Registration

Dear Encounter Participant,

We are so excited that you will be attending the Encounter Weekend [month dates, year], at [Name of Retreat Center] in [Town], [State]! This letter will provide the details for the weekend. Please read ALL the sections.

Cancellation policy: Life happens and things come up. You may cancel with full refund until [Day, Month date]. From [Month date] through [Month date], you will receive a half refund. After [Month date], there will be no refund. If a cancellation is due to COVID, a refund of the cost minus a $25 administrative fee will be issued.

Arrival: Please plan to arrive at [Retreat Center] between 6:15 and 7:00 pm for registration. This will give you a chance to find your room before the program starts at 7:00 pm. There is no evening meal Friday, so please plan to eat dinner prior to your arrival or bring a bagged meal. Light snacks will be provided later in the evening and throughout the weekend.

Address:

[Name of Retreat Center

Street address

Town, State, zip code]

[Name of Retreat Center] has its own liability waiver, which you will sign upon arrival. It also has a strict no pet policy. If you rely on a support animal, please notify Encounter immediately. The pet must be approved by [Name of Retreat Center] before it can be brought onto the property.

What to bring: Bible, journal, pen, sleeping bag or bedding, pillow, towel, toiletries, etc. The facility has sheets and towels to rent, which are $10.00/person. If you need linens, please bring $10.00 with you (we can't do debit cards) and let us know at registration. We will collect your money and direct you to the linen closet. If you tend to sleep on the cooler side, definitely consider bringing an extra blanket.

Room temperatures can vary throughout the facility, and at least one of our sessions will take place outdoors, weather permitting. We suggest that you dress in layers or bring along a sweater as well as coat. We wish everyone to be comfortable so they can hear from God without distraction. Also for that reason we ask that for everyone's health/comfort that you do not wear perfumes or other strong scented creams, etc. during the weekend.

Get lost/Break down/Going to be late: Give us a call if you are going to arrive late. We don't want to worry about you and are here to help you find your way. You can call or text [Encounter Administrator] at [phone number].

———

We are so excited about what God has in store for us all this weekend and can't wait for our time together to begin. We have been preparing and praying for this time and specifically for you for several months. God is ready to meet each of us in a very personal and beautiful way!

Please direct any questions you might have to [your encounter administrator] at [encounter administrator's e-mail address]. May God bless you as you prepare for your upcoming Encounter Weekend!

Blessings,

[Encounter Director]

Sample Testimony Preparation Letter

Preparing Your Testimony: Encounter Warfare

Dear _____,

Welcome to the journey of preparing and presenting your testimony, along with teaching a session, at an Encounter Weekend! Testifying not only releases the power of the Kingdom unto others' transformation but is an important part of maintaining the freedom that you personally have received. You will grow in confidence in the Lord's power at work in your own life to deliver you from sin and keep you pure. Please be sure to read all instructions carefully and use the guiding questions and time constraints as a guide as you craft your testimony. Once your testimony is written out (preferably within two weeks of an upcoming Encounter), email me so that we can come up with a time to meet, either live or via zoom, so that I can pray for and with you, and offer you any help you might need in making finishing touches on your session. I look forward to ministering alongside you and also to seeing what the Lord will accomplish as you step out in courage and faith and share with others what He has done.

Blessings,

Rev. Amy Howard*

Director, Encounter Culture

Anglican Diocese of New England

[*Fill in the name of your Encounter Director and ministry, if applicable, in lieu of ours]

1. Releasing the Power of Your Testimony

Please use the following questions to shape your testimony. Resist the temptation to "teach"—simply share your story.

- What have you been set free from? *Name the sin.*
- How did the sin impact your life? Relationships? Prayer? *Be specific.*
- Who was hurt by your sin? *What happened?*
- How did you come to realize it was sin?
- What did God do for you? *How are you changed?*

If your testimony involves your parents, remember:

- All people (parents) are broken.
- All parents wound their children.

Hopefully, one day your children will be testifying of their own freedom from parent wounds.

Own all personal sin. There are two tendencies when dealing with parental wounds: the first is denial (particularly in Christian communities). The second is laying the blame for personal sin on parents (permanent victim, psychologizing sin).

2. Basic Guidelines for Presentations

- Please keep your session (notes and slides along with your testimony) to no more than 30 minutes in length; this will leave ample time for ministry.
- Prepare your lesson according to the PowerPoint slides and notes assigned to you and incorporate your own personal story. Do not make any changes without permission from [Encounter Director]. We ask that all notes are read as written, without preaching or editing, unless otherwise discussed with the Encounter Director.

Be sure to understand and know all material provided on your assigned PowerPoint. If you have any questions in regards to your session, please feel free to ask. We want you to feel confident in what you're presenting.

Now unto him that is able to keep you from falling, and to present you faultless before the presence of his glory with exceeding joy,

To the only wise God our Saviour, be glory and majesty, dominion and power, both now and ever. Amen.

Jude 1:24-25 (KJV)

Prayer Ministers' Contract, Ministry Team Contract

Dear Encounter Prayer Minister,

It is an absolute pleasure to have you join us for such a time as this and look forward to having your participation in future events. For the purposes of clearly defining your role and responsibilities, our expectations, and the liabilities, we ask that you carefully read through and sign and date the contract of agreement provided below.

The best and often only necessary advertisement for an Encounter Weekend are people who've already been to one and experienced the transforming, healing power of testimony, confession and prayer. To that end, we ask that each ministry team member try their utmost to bring along at least one friend or acquaintance who has never been to an Encounter Weekend. I encourage you to use this as an opportunity to share the good news (and a great weekend!) with someone who might otherwise be too busy, nervous, distracted, or simply uninformed.

All team members are expected to honor their time commitment(s) according to the event and give the adequate notice, of 1 month prior to event date, of any changes or inability to attend.

Dress Code: Smart Casual (no sweatpants, gym attire etc.)

Teachers:

- Prepare accordingly to the session you have been assigned.

- Make all necessary arrangements to see that you are successful in every area of your assigned session.

- Keep your session 30 min in length, including the time it takes to share your testimony; this will leave ample time for ministry.

- Prepare your session according to the PowerPoint slides and notes assigned to you and incorporate your own personal story in the section marked "testimony". Do not make any changes without permission from [NAME of ENCOUNTER LEADER].

- Be sure to understand and know all material provided on your assigned PowerPoint. If you have any questions in regard to your session, please feel free to ask. We want you to feel confident in what you're presenting.

Note: All team members are expected to attend *all* sessions.

We strongly encourage each minister to make every effort to invite and bring at least one participant to the Encounter at which they will be ministering. This gives team members the opportunity to share some of their story and invite others to receive as well. Begin asking the Lord about who to bring well in advance of the Encounter at which you will be ministering so that you're not scrambling at the last minute.

Confidentiality Agreement: Due to the nature of a God Encounter Weekend, you will find yourself in a position where attendees and other volunteers will share information with you regarding their personal lives, both past and present, disabilities, etc. You are required to respect the privacy of all individuals during this event, and to hold in confidence all information obtained in the course of service. Information which could be life-threatening to the attendee, or by the attendee to another, should be divulged, and then only with the Ministry Team Coordinator (or other appropriate professionals).

If ever an individual shares information with you which makes you feel uncomfortable or if there is ever any doubt as to the propriety of sharing information, please consult with the Ministry Team Coordinator or other appropriate supervisor.

Any breach of confidentiality will be dealt with under the discretion of the Ministry Team Coordinator or other appropriate supervisor and may result in the revoking of all current and future participation to serve at this event.

It is important for volunteers to be clear about their own limits with those they represent, so that they do not find themselves in positions where they are hearing information they would prefer not to hear, or if they feel that they are not able to keep within the boundaries of confidentiality.

I hereby agree to hold all information pertaining to any recipient as confidential unless asked in writing by the recipient to share this information with another, or in any life-threatening situation.

I agree to meet all required expectations:

Volunteer signature: _____

Date: _____

APPENDIX 5

Sample Housekeeping Announcements

- Please read the information on the dressers in your room – it explains the heat. If you turn the heat on, please remember to turn it off.
- You may use both bathrooms on the third floor.
- Noise carries on the upper level–please remember others may be sleeping.
- Do not remake your bed–when you leave just fold your blanket at the bottom. Leave your sheets on the bed.
- Place used towels and washcloths in the hampers in the bathroom. They will be laundered on Saturday and returned for your use.
- Extra blankets/pillows/towels are located in the closet across from room #2.
- The second floor is home to residents who stay onsite. Please do not enter that level unless you are going to a Ministry Team meeting.
- Snacks are always available in the back of the room. Help yourself.
- The doors lock at dusk–if you need to go outside, arrange to have someone let you back in.
- Breakfast is served at 8:00 am. Coffee will be available by 6:30 am.
- Hot water availability is improved but still is limited if everyone takes a shower in the morning. Please keep this in mind and plan accordingly.
- If you have any other questions concerning the facility, please come find me.

Encounter Materials Checklist

✔	Item	Amount
	Cash Box with Cash	1
	Pens	#R*
	Tissue Boxes	6–8
	Mints	Large bag
	Tape or poster gum	1
	Tablecloths (opt. for purchase with logo)	2
	Signage (weekend schedule, welcome banner)	optional
	Earplugs for participants	Large bag
	Nametag lanyards w/nametag holders	#R
	Laptop for registration, PowerPoint	1
	Laptop for room prophecies	1–2
	"Blue" binder:	1
	–Encounter transaction input form	
	–Session notes	
	–Director handbook	
	–Administrator handbook	
	–Weekend apprentice schedule	
	–Ministry assignments, setup schedule	
	–Additional prayers (Cutting Free, etc.)	
	Spiritual Profiles	#R
	Participant Handbooks	#R
	Blessed oil for anointing	6–8
	Passion DVD or digital clip	
	Cross	1

	Nails	#R +10
	Hammers	3
	Fire pit (if there isn't one on site)	1
	Logs, kindling, newspaper for fire	
	Lighter/matches	
	Suggested Donation signage	3
	T-shirts, journals, other book table items	optional

* #R is the number of registered attendees.

Apprentice Schedule

Session	Apprentice	Prayer Minister
Come Like Peter		
Sin/The Cross		
Healing Our Image of God		
Sexual Wholeness		
Keys of the Kingdom		

Be Filled		

APPENDIX 7B
Ministry Team Assignments

Name	Session	Function	Set Up	Small Group
1.	Come Like Peter			
2.	Sin			
3.	The Cross			
4.	Healing Our Image of God			
5.	Sexual Wholeness: Men			
6.	Sexual Wholeness: Women			
7.	Keys of the Kingdom			
8.	Be Filled			
9.	Run With the Vision			

Name	Session	Function	Set Up	Small Group
10.				
11.				
12.				
13.				
14.				
15.				
16.				
17.				
18.				

Name	Session	Function	Set Up	Small Group
19.				
20.				
21.				
22.				
23.				
24.				
25.				
26.				
27.				

APPENDIX 7C

Encounter Registration Form

First Name	Last Name	Birthdate	Gender	Phone #	Room #	Small Group #	Function	Emergency Contact	Balance Due	Dietary Allergies

Encounter Transaction Input Form

Date:_____

Location:_____

Encounter Administrator:_____

Codes:	400	Registration
	403	Merchandise
	407	Financial Donations

Type of Transaction	Code	Quantity	Amount	Paid by (Cash, check #, credit card*)
			$	
			$	
			$	
			$	
			$	
			$	
			$	
			$	
			$	
			$	
			$	
			$	
			$	
			$	
			$	
			$	
			$	

*Donations to Encounter Culture, registration payments, and checks for merchandise should be made out to ADNE, with "Encounter Culture" noted in the memo.

Encounter Director Handbook

Friday

Ministry Team Meeting (before Encounter begins)

1. **Group introduction,** identify intercessors.

2. **Give an overview** of the role of a prayer minister:

Do:	• Listen to the person who would like prayer and to the Holy Spirit • Ask permission to place a hand on their head/shoulder before prayer • If you're going to be silent and wait on the Lord, let the recipient know why you're quiet
Don't:	• Use insider language when interviewing or praying • Offer advice or counsel to "fix" problems • Release your personal information such as phone number, e-mail address unless approved by Encounter Director • Worry about getting through everything the first night! • Worry at all

3. **Remind ministers to explain,** when necessary, the importance of speaking renunciations out loud and commanding the enemy to go. The enemy can't read their minds.

4. **If people want to confess session-specific stuff**, encourage them to wait until after that session, because they may have more clarity to help them process. Ask whether they would like to wait and minister accordingly.

5. **Inform the team that if any of them (the team) need prayer,** they are welcome and encouraged to speak to the lead intercessor or to grab

another prayer minister to pray with. Ministers are always on some level recipients as well as ministers and may nail sins to the cross during the cross session, fill out a profile and receive a new name if they wish.

6. **Keep in mind** that whether someone sinned against you, or you sinned against someone else or yourself: if you can call it sin, you can get set free from it.

7. **Be mindful of the difference** between grief and unforgiveness. Some people may need to feel the legitimacy of their grief, or permission to grieve, and this is not the same thing as unforgiveness. Forgiveness is an act of will; healing is a gift from God; both can take time to process (and the process sometimes involves grief).

8. **Read the Apprentice Schedule**; introduce Apprentices to their Prayer Ministers for the Friday evening session.

9. **Remind Session Leader** that their session only lasts 30 minutes.

10. **Prayer** for Come Like Peter presenter, Emcee, Worship Leader

11. **Prayers of Protection**

Worship (Encounter begins)

Conference Announcements (following worship):

1. **Welcome!** We are so glad that you are here. Our vision for you this weekend is to see you set free by the power of the Holy Spirit and released to walk in the fullness of your identity as son/daughter of God.

2. **Introductions:** introduce who people are and what their titles are: Encounter Director, Emcee (if different from Director), Encounter Administrator, ministry team. Make distinction between those wearing ministry tags and participant tags.

3. **Housekeeping Items**

4. **Weekend Announcements:**

   a) If you are not on the prayer team, don't minister to anyone else. This is about you, and we want to help you to receive, rather than give. Many of you are capable ministers, but this is about you. Sometimes we are inclined to use ministry toward others as a way out of being honest and vulnerable with our own brokenness.

   b) Avoid comforting other participants out of an experience with God. If you see someone crying, journaling, etc., give them space to hear from God.

   c) Sessions build on one another throughout the weekend—it's best to attend them all rather than pick the ones which seem interesting

   d) After the first teaching session, there will be a time for prayer.

5. **Opening Prayer**

"Come Like Peter" session

Conference Announcements:

1. Introduce time of prayer ministry: what is it, how it will function. Welcome them to receive prayer multiple times from as many Prayer Ministers as desired.

2. Introduce Prayer Ministers and tell how they got to be ministers at Encounter: everyone has been to an Encounter, been through training, and has signed an agreement of confidentiality.

3. Make mention of the 4 R's.

4. Remind attendees not to comfort anyone out of their own experience of God or the conviction of the Holy Spirit: If you see your friend upset, leave them to be with the Lord.

5. Introduce them to profiles and booklets. After receiving prayer, take time to fill out what you want to get out of the weekend, and begin to fill out profiles—be honest!

Prayer Ministry

1. Read room prophecies

2. Introduce small group leaders, break up into small groups

Saturday

Ministry Team Meeting (Saturday before breakfast)

1. **Remind Prayer Ministers to give people homework:**

   a) Sin Session break: write out the sin that has been holding them back from the Lord (they will nail this to the cross).

   b) During Sexual session and Closing Doors: If they had a long list of sexual partners, write out each name. Of they can't remember names, be as specific as possible (i.e., "The redhead I met at the bar").

2. **If somebody seems "stuck,"** especially at the Closing Doors session, ask them if they've been involved in any occult activity either as a child or recently. Have them bring their profiles with them and have them deal with the occult stuff first.

3. **If someone is working their way through the 4 R's but they keep praying, "Take this away from me,"** coach them to say "I repent," or "I renounce."

4. **Prayer Ministers should grab 4 R cards to hand out** during prayer ministry and explain cards to the participants.

5. **Prayer for Sin and Cross session leaders**

6. **Prayers for Protection and Cutting Free after ministry**

Worship

"Sin" session

Short break, no prayer ministry. Stay in a prayerful place, write down the sin that has been holding you back from the Lord.

Conference Announcements:

1. **Inform** group that they are going to watch a short video and that following the video they will be given the opportunity to come down front, nail their sins to the cross, pick up a new name (the first one they take, not sifting through), and receive prayer.

2. **Introduce** the James 5 reality of confessing sins to one another for healing, and let the group know that there will be Prayer Ministers available to minister to them once they have nailed their sins to the cross.

3. **Invite** Prayer Ministers to be ready to take their places following the video.

"The Cross" session (before *Passion* clip)

Passion clip

Ministry time

Lunch: Pray Blessing on the meal

Ministry Team Meeting (Saturday after lunch)

1. **Prayers for protection and cutting free after ministry**

2. **Debrief:** How is everyone doing?

3. **Pray** for "Healing Our Image of God" presenter and "Sexual Purity" presenter

Worship

"Healing Our Image of God" session

Conference Announcements:

1. Introduce orphan/sonship chart

2. Introduce Mother/Father Identificational Repentance*

3. Encourage people to come for a blessing and receive prayer ministry

For Mother and Father Identificational Repentance, we use the identificational prayers crafted by Christian Healing Ministries. They can be found at christian-healingmin.org, under the "Resources" dropdown.

Ministry Time

Conference Announcements:

1. **Announce** the break

2. **Bring profiles** to the next session

Break

"Sexual Wholeness" session

Ministry Time

Conference Announcements:

1. **Remind small groups** that they will eat together for dinner

2. **Bring coats,** appropriate shoes to next session

3. **Let participants know that there will be an opportunity to give** to Encounter ministry tomorrow

4. **Remind people** about the book table

Dinner: Pray blessing on the meal

Ministry Team Meeting (Saturday after dinner)

1. **Cutting Free prayer, Prayer for Protection**

2. **Debrief**

3. **Receive update from Lead Intercessor**

4. **Divide people into groups for ministry time:** physical healing group, identify deliverance ministry help

5. **Identify people who are going to set up for "freedom ministry" time** (dancing, fire pit, or whatever you have planned)

6. **Identify fire starters**—the fire will need to be started 20 minutes before the end of ministry time. Start the fire with all of the pieces of paper removed from the cross. If you will be having someone else lead the time by the fire, make sure they know who they are.

7. **Pray** for "Keys of the Kingdom" presenter

Worship

"Keys of the Kingdom" session

Conference Announcements:

1. **Encourage participants to bring their profiles** when receiving prayer ministry

2. **Remind participants not to leave** following ministry time.

Ministry Time

- **Fire Time:** Make sure to remind participants to bring profiles outside. Encounter Director may lead Fire Time, or delegate to another prayer minister. At the fire, offer participants and prayer ministers time to throw their profiles in the fire, state their new name, and offer a 30-second testimony regarding what they've been set free from.

- **Freedom Ministry Time:** Dance, fire time, or other desired activity.

Sunday

Ministry Team Meeting (Sunday before breakfast)

Prayers of Protection and Cutting Free after ministry

1. **Continue to pray** for anyone who still seems to be stuck.

2. **Ask:** Are there men/women that need to get saved?

3. **Remind others** that often people let go of their junk in the Holy Spirit session.

4. **Go over logistics** for set up of prayer ministry—if you will be organizing an area for physical healing prayer, what you're inviting people to receive prayer for, etc.

5. **Have ministers break up into teams of two;** give oil to each team.

6. **Remind ministers of the three questions:**
   - Can we anoint you?
   - Can we place our hands on your shoulders/head?
   - Are you comfortable if we pray in our prayer language?

7. **Have ministers encourage participants to hold open hands** when receiving, and have participants themselves (if they wish) ask the Holy Spirit to come.

8. **Don't be afraid to wait on the Holy Spirit** for infilling, for words of knowledge, for healing.

9. **Encourage prayer ministers to ask** each one if they have received the gift of a prayer language; if not (and they would like them to), pray for them to receive.

Breakfast: Pray for the meal

Worship

"Holy Spirit" session

Conference Announcements:

1. **Invite anyone** who would like a fresh or initial baptism of the Holy Spirit to come receive ministry.

2. **Encourage participants to receive ministry** for any remaining issues that the Holy Spirit has brought up.

Ministry Time

"Run With the Vision" session

Conference Announcements:

1. **Note resources available**—book table will close before lunch, promotional materials, how to sign up for future Encounter Culture Events, etc.

2. **How and why to give** to Encounter Culture

3. **Closing Housekeeping** announcements

4. **Let participants know** that we will be doing testimonies during lunch

5. **Prayer** for lunch

Lunch, testimonies

Cutting free prayer with ministers, intercessors

APPENDIX 7f
Encounter Administrator Guide

Date:_____

Location:_____

Encounter Administrator:_____

1. The Encounter Administrator is in charge of packing for an Encounter Weekend. A complete list of supplies needed can be found in Appendix 6 of the *How to Run an Encounter Weekend Manual*. Once you arrive at your Encounter Weekend, the Administrator will oversee the placement and usage of the following items: cash box, Registration forms and Registration check-in, Receipt Form, and the inventory of items for sale (t-shirts, journals, Kingdom books, etc.)

2. Display all the items for sale on a table and include a "Suggested Donation" tag for the items displayed.

3. Using the Registration Check-In form, check off the names of the individuals coming in. Check to see if they have paid for their registration. If they have not paid for their registration, or have an unpaid balance, collect the appropriate funds and update the Receipt form. If some of your participants have received scholarships, be aware that this may affect their unpaid balance if the scholarships have not yet been applied.

4. Walk-ins without a previous registration need to be processed according to the procedure listed under 3, if space at the Encounter facility remains available, and you have the approval of your Encounter Director. Manually insert their name on the Registration Check-In form, and update the Receipt form to record their payment

5. Keep track of and record all donations and sales of items on the Receipt form throughout the weekend. Keep all funds collected in the cash box, which should remain locked when not in use and safely placed in a secured location.

6. At the end of the weekend, return the cash box (containing all funds collected, completed Receipt form and Registration Check-In form), and all unsold items to the Encounter Director. The Encounter Director will turn over the locked cash box to the treasurer for banking processing.

Additional Prayers

For Wisdom: Ephesians 1:17–19a

"I keep asking that the God of our Lord Jesus Christ, the glorious Father, may give you the Spirit of wisdom and revelation, so that you may know him better. I pray that the eyes of your heart may be enlightened in order that you may know the hope to which he has called you, the riches of his glorious inheritance in his holy people, and his incomparably great power for us who believe."

For Strength: Ephesians 3:14–19

"For this reason I kneel before the Father, from whom every family in heaven and on earth derives its name. I pray that out of his glorious riches he may strengthen you with power through his Spirit in your inner being, so that Christ may dwell in your hearts through faith. And I pray that you, being rooted and established in love, may have power, together with all the Lord's holy people, to grasp how wide and long and high and deep is the love of Christ, and to know this love that surpasses knowledge—that you may be filled to the measure of all the fullness of God."

For Knowledge and Insight: Philippians 1:9–11

"And this is my prayer: that your love may abound more and more in knowledge and depth of insight, so that you may be able to discern what is best and may be pure and blameless for the day of Christ, filled with the fruit of righteousness that comes through Jesus Christ—to the glory and praise of God."

For Love: 1 Thessalonians 3:11–13

"Now may our God and Father himself and our Lord Jesus clear the way for us to come to you. May the Lord make your love increase and overflow for each other and for everyone else, just as ours does for you. May he strengthen your hearts so that you will be blameless and holy in the presence of our God and Father when our Lord Jesus comes with all his holy ones."

For Boldness: Acts 4:29–30

"Now, Lord, consider their threats and enable your servants to speak your word with great boldness. Stretch out your hand to heal and perform signs and wonders through the name of your holy servant Jesus."

A Personal Prayer for the Beginning of a Healing Process or Journey

"God, my systems are broken. My body, and mind, and will, and emotions hurt in ways I cannot fix. Sometimes I care, and sometimes I don't. Sometimes I want to be fixed, and sometimes I just think that the process would be too hard, or hurt to badly, or be too disruptive, and might not make things better anyway. Sometimes I feel unworthy of being healed; like I deserve to suffer. Or maybe I think that at least suffering brings me some of the love and attention that I am so empty of, and so I don't even want to be healed. Or maybe it's been too long, and I've seen too much, and I am too tired or angry or sad to try any more. Jesus, I need more than what I have. Change me, so that I want to want your love more than what I have settled for. Give me the courage to see what is true, and to follow you wherever you lead me. Come, Holy Spirit, and bring the Kingdom of the Father." [1]

A Prayer for Protection, to be Prayed Before Ministry

In the name of Jesus Christ of Nazareth, the Son of God who came in the flesh, and by the power of His cross and his blood, we bind up the power of any evil spirits and command them to be silent, bound from interfering in any way in our ministry or prayers. We bind up the evil powers and spirits working or sent against us in the mighty name of Jesus Christ of Nazareth. We break any curses, hexes or spells sent against us and declare them null and void. We break the assignments of any spirits sent against us and send them to Jesus to deal with them as He will. Lord, we ask You to bless our enemies by sending Your Holy

---

[1] Amy Howard, *The Pain Eaters*, 2021.

Spirit to lead them to repentance and conversion. We ask for the protection of the shed blood of Jesus Christ over _____.

Thank You, Lord, for Your protection and for sending Your warring angels to help us in the battle. We ask You to guide us in our prayers and to share with us Your Spirit's power and compassion with us. Amen. [2]

A Prayer Following Ministry, for Cleansing and Renewal

Lord Jesus, thank You for sharing with us Your wonderful ministry of healing and deliverance. Thank You for Your healing—the healings we have witnessed today, and all healing that we cannot yet see. We realize that the sickness and evil we encounter is more than our humanity can bear, so cleanse us of any sadness, negativity, or despair that we may have picked up. If our ministry has tempted us to anger, impatience or lust, cleanse us of those temptations and replace them with love, joy, and peace. If any evil spirits have attached themselves to us or oppressed us in any way, we command them to depart—now—and go straight to Jesus Christ for Him to deal with you as He will.

Come Holy Spirit: renew us—fill us anew with Your power, Your life and Your joy. Strengthen us where we have felt weak and clothe us with Your light. Fill us with life. Lord Jesus, please send your Your holy angels to minister to us and our families—guard us and protect us from all sickness, harm, and accidents. (Give us a safe trip home.) We praise you You now and forever, Father, Son and Holy Spirit, and we ask these things in Jesus' Holy Name that he He may be glorified. Amen. [3]

A Prayer to be Set Free From Co-Dependency

"Lord, I want my joy, my deep sense of well-being, to be free. It is wound around [name(s)]. I cannot fix them, or save them, or prevent their pain. I choose right now to give You each of these people, their pain, their happiness, their entire lives, and I cut free from them in the mighty name of Jesus Christ. I hand to You, at the cross, my guilt for failing them, my judgments of myself and others, my anger and resentment, and theirs. (Feel free to add any other sin, pain, or

---

[2] Inspired by the prayer of protection from Christian Healing Ministry, available at Christianhealingmin.org

[3] Modified from a prayer from Christian Healing Ministry, available at Christianhealingmin. org

injuries to your prayer here, and release each of them, by name, to the One who loves you best.) Come, friend, and heal my soul where it has been wounded by carrying things and people that were too heavy for me. Thank You for freedom. I love You." [4]

For Health of Body and Soul

"May God the Father bless you, God the Son heal you, God the Holy Spirit give you strength. May God the holy and undivided Trinity guard your body, save your soul, and bring you safely to his heavenly country; where he lives and reigns for ever and ever. Amen." [5]

---

[4] Amy Howard, *The Pain Eaters*, 2021.
[5] From *The Book of Common Prayer* (Anglican Liturgy Press, 2019), 233.

APPENDIX 7H
Questions to Provoke Celebration, Thanksgiving, and Growth

1. *What did I enjoy most about this journey?*

2. *What did I do well? What strengths did I use?*

3. *What skills did I gain?*

4. *What do I feel most confident about?*

5. *Were there obstacles that I overcame?*

6. *How did I do it?*

7. *Where was God in this for me?*

Part III

Session Notes

Come Like Peter

Slide 1 – Come Like Peter

When Jesus began His ministry on earth, He picked out 12 everyday guys to be His closest followers, His disciples. In those days, any teacher of the holy scriptures (called a rabbi) would pick followers to live with him and he would teach them everything he knew about God and living a holy life. It was a great honor and privilege in that society to be a disciple of a rabbi. When Jesus the Rabbi chose His disciples, one of them was Simon, a rough and tough fisherman. The Bible describes Simon as impulsive, quick to speak or act and think later, overenthusiastic, brash, emotional, passionate. This was not a typical first pick for a serious disciple of a rabbi. However, he was one of the first picks of Jesus. When Jesus looked at Simon, He saw an honest, humble man with strong faith in God. He also saw something else in Simon that Simon didn't see in himself. Jesus looked at him and said, "So you are Simon, the son of John? **You will be called Peter** (which means rock)."

Jesus changed Simon's name when He first met him, in a way that was prophesying over Simon's life. Jesus was "calling that which was not, as though it were." He saw something that wasn't even true about Simon at the time, but that would be true about him in the future.

Slide 2 – What's In a Name?

Changing people's names was something God had done before in the Bible. Why? Whenever God changes someone's name, it is to give that person a **new identity** and a **new mission**.

For example, in Genesis, God made a covenant with a man named **Abram**. A covenant is about two people joining together so completely that that each take on the identity of the other with all the corresponding benefits and responsibilities. Abram became identified as belonging to *Yahweh* (the Lord) when God gave Abram and his wife Sarai the two "h's" from his sacred name and made their names Abraham and Sarah. They received a new *identity*, and their new *mission* was to produce offspring that would bless the nations—Jesus would be born thousands of years later in their family line.

God changed Abraham's grandson **Jacob**'s name – his name meant "liar, deceiver," and he lived into that name. But in his encounter with God, when he wrestled with the angel, God gave him the new name of *Israel*, which means "to strive with God." This was a name of great honor because he did make every effort and he obtained a great blessing from God. He had a new *identity*, and his new *mission* was to carry on Abraham's mission and establish a great people with great blessing.

Not long after Jesus started calling Simon "Rock," or "Peter," Jesus miraculously provided a massive catch of fish to Peter and the other fisherman in Luke Chapter 5. The fishnets were breaking and the boats were sinking under the weight of so many fish! Peter and the others were quickly aware and awed at the fact that Jesus was not an ordinary man, and Peter was overwhelmed with humility, bowing down to exclaim that Jesus was God, without even helping the others get the fish into the boat!

Here is where Jesus gives him his new mission. Luke 5:10–11 tells us: "Then Jesus said to Simon, 'Don't be afraid; **from now on you will fish for people**.' So they pulled their boats up on shore, left everything and followed him." Jesus spent the next three years traveling around the country of Israel, teaching His 12 disciples and the immense crowds that started to follow them about God's character, His Kingdom, and His plan for their redemption. He miraculously healed people wherever He went, and as He became more and more famous and popular, there was a lot of controversy over who Jesus really was. Not everyone believed He was God's son. In Matthew chapter 16, when Jesus asked the disciples who they thought He was, Peter responded quickly (I'm reading from *The Message* Bible):

> *"You are the Christ, the Messiah, the Son of the living God."*
> *And Jesus answered him, "God bless you, Simon, son of John!*
> *You didn't get that answer out of books or from teachers. My*
> *Father in heaven, God himself, let you in on this secret of*
> *who I really am. And now I'm going to tell you who you really*
> *are. You **are** Peter, a rock. This is the rock on which I will put*
> *together my church, a church so expansive with energy that*

not even the gates of hell will be able to keep it out. "And that's not all. You will have complete and free access to God's kingdom, keys to open any and every door: no more barriers between heaven and earth, earth and heaven. A yes on earth is yes in heaven. A no on earth is no in heaven."

Notice that when Jesus and Simon met for the first time, Jesus had said, "You *will* be called Peter, a rock." But at Peter's exclamation of faith that Jesus is the Messiah, it is no longer a "you will be called," but, as Jesus exclaims, "you *are* Peter." Jesus' prophecy about Peter, something Peter couldn't see in the beginning but something Jesus saw all along, was fulfilled—he was to be the "rock."

Have you ever heard God described as a "Rock"? Many times in the Old Testament, God is referred to as a rock, and Jesus identified himself with the name *Rock* in the Sermon on the Mount. Essentially, because this gift of faith from the Father revealed the true identity of Jesus to Peter, Jesus was saying that Peter now shared Jesus' identity. Peter was now a fully adopted part of the family. The Father and the Son have received Peter into their fellowship, and Peter has become one with them in a covenant of faith. Jesus' exclamation that Peter has been "given keys to the kingdom of heaven" means that Jesus gave Peter access to all that belonged to Him, all the power and authority, Jesus as the Son of the King of the Universe.

This is a mind-blowing reality that also applies to you and me: When we are saved, when we declare from deep in our heart as Peter did that Jesus is the Son of God, the Savior and Lord, we become one with Jesus through that faith. First Corinthians 12:8 declares that this kind of strong faith in the core of our being is a gift from God. With this faith that Jesus is Lord, we receive in our identity everything Jesus has, including the relationship Jesus enjoys with the Father. We belong to God's fellowship, and the Holy Spirit is a seal, guaranteeing that relationship forever!

So, Peter was one of the closest friends of Jesus, he received his identity and mission from Jesus, and he had been nurtured by Jesus the rabbi for 3 years. He was in, and he was loyal! But after many tests of Peter's love and commitment to Jesus, Peter failed what was perhaps his greatest test. Jesus' ministry gained popularity and He was a famous celebrity in the whole country, but things took a turn for the worse after increasing opposition from powerful Jewish leaders. Jesus was arrested on charges of blasphemy for saying that He was God—which almost certainly meant death, and death not only for Jesus, but quite possibly for His closest followers as well. Peter was scared.

While Jesus was on trial in front of the Jewish leaders, three different people asked Peter, "Hey, aren't you one of Jesus' buddies?" And three times He answered, "I swear, I don't even know Him."

And the Lord turned and looked at Peter. And Peter remembered the saying of the Lord, how he had said to him, "Before the rooster crows today, you will deny me three times." And Peter went out and wept bitterly. (Luke 22:61–62)

Slide 3 – Sources of Shame

This unthinkable failure, in the ultimate test of Peter's covenant relationship with Jesus, right before Jesus' crucifixion, overwhelmed Peter with shame. He wept bitterly! He assumed he was disqualified from carrying on Jesus' ministry, and he went back to what he was good at— fishing. Early one morning, shortly after Jesus' resurrection, the disciples were out fishing on the sea and a man appeared on the shore and greeted them. Suddenly their nets were full with a miraculous amount of fish. They had seen this before! When Peter realized the man on the shore was Jesus, he jumped out and swam to the shore, leaving the rest of the fishermen to pull the fish into the boat. He must have known Jesus' character well enough that he knew Jesus would be excited to see him. And then they all had breakfast with Jesus on the shore.

Slide 4 – Peter

From John 21:15—After breakfast, Jesus took Peter on a walk alone. He asked Peter three times, "Do you love me?" Peter was frustrated that Jesus didn't seem to be listening when he answered, "Yes, of course I love you!"

Jesus didn't ask Peter the question, "Do you love me?" for information because Jesus didn't know the answer. Jesus asked to bring out Peter's confidence in the truth: "Let me tell you something about yourself that you can't see—you *do* love me, Peter."

Slide 5 – 3 Denials and 3 Affirmations

The picture we have of Jesus here is not what we might expect from someone who had been completely betrayed by a friend in His time of greatest need: He didn't make sure Peter knew He was disappointed with his performance. He didn't admonish or chastise Peter, or withhold love and acceptance until Peter demonstrated adequate repentance for his sin. No, instead we see a Jesus bubbling over with the joy at the chance to *forgive* Peter, to *heal* and *restore* him! Peter's shame was all washed away as Jesus brought him to a solid, unshakable confidence in who he really was: that he *was* a man after God's own heart, that he *did*, in fact, *love* Jesus, and that he *was* called by Jesus to do *great* things. His identity and mission were reestablished with unshakable confidence by an *encounter* with the risen Christ.

Slide 6 – Come Expecting

That is what this Encounter God weekend is for you, now, too.

Jesus wants to meet with you here, and He will, if you come like Peter. Here are some ways to do that: you can write it in your booklet.

1. **Come Expecting** – When Peter jumped out of the boat into the water, he was thrilled to be in Jesus' presence again, full of faith that Jesus still loved him. Faith as small as a mustard seed is adequate to move an entire mountain. Bring your faith, whatever size it is, to Jesus, and come this weekend expecting that Jesus sees your potential in His Kingdom, and that He is calling you to fulfill that destiny. Come expecting to receive from Jesus.

2. **Come Alone** – After they ate breakfast with the others, Peter and Jesus went for a walk alone to talk one on one. This weekend is for you to do that: **focus** on restoring your relationship with the one who loves you the most! How do we come alone with Jesus, with all these people around?

   a) Be focused and be present to Jesus – turn off cell phones and computers during the sessions and choose above all to **engage** with God.

   b) Remember that you are not here to minister to others. Don't pray for others – just receive.

153

c) Don't worry about others, here or at home. Spending this weekend focused on Jesus is the most loving thing you can do for your family and friends right now, even if it feels selfish.

3. **Come Hungry** – Peter jumped out of the boat and left the others to bring in the fish! He couldn't wait to be with Jesus. Whatever he was so hungry for, he got more than he bargained for... total freedom from the heavy shame he'd been carrying, and a totally new way to view himself and God.

    What do you want from God? Write it down in your book. Freedom from addiction, depression or self-hatred? Do you want Jesus to give you identity, purpose, or healing? Why have you jumped out of your boat to be here this weekend?

    "Blessed are those who hunger and thirst for righteousness for they shall be filled" (Matthew 5:6). Are you hungry for more of God? That means you're healthy. What kind of people are not hungry? Sick people. If your spiritual lethargy has eclipsed your hunger, there is a problem: you are not well. So, ask God for hunger.

    Perhaps you're a Christian who has been stuck in a way of sin for so long that, logically, your spiritual imagination has really shrunk. God seems so tiny. You can no longer conceive of a God who is desirable or powerful.

    Maybe you don't feel hunger for God because you're so hurt and wounded by your past or present failures that you have disqualified yourself, or you're too afraid to hope for something more because you're unworthy, or you're afraid God won't come through the way you want him to. In the authority of the Living God, I say to you tonight: "There is hope, and there is more."

    Whether you are feeling voraciously hungry for more of God this weekend, or whether you don't know why you don't have desire, it's okay. The good news is that you can pray, and God **will** show you! After I'm done talking, the prayer ministers will be coming up to the front, and you are invited to come up and just pray for hunger for this weekend.

4. **Come Willing to Be Broken** – In order for Peter to get what he really wanted, he had to be **vulnerable** enough to have the conversation with Jesus about sin, shame, and regret. Ouch! Remember that Jesus did this

gently, referring to the three denials by encouraging Peter to forgive himself by moving on into the truest thing about himself: that he was loved by God and was a sincere lover of God. That he had a new identity, and a new mission.

We have to be willing to expose our shame and let the Lord into the most painful and shameful memories we have. We need to let him into specific events, things we've done and things that were done to us that we haven't forgotten but have served to drive us into insecurity, isolation, anger, bitterness, and pride.

We need to allow God to reopen wounds, no matter how painful. When a broken bone has been set wrong, it needs to be re-broken and reset by a capable doctor. It is a painful process, but it is necessary for true healing to begin. Even after his most profound failure, Peter was willing to come face-to-face with Jesus about the past, he was willing to face the hurt. Be brave. God is a true healer. Come willing to be broken.

5. **Come Real** – Peter came real before God. Even though just being in the presence of Jesus must have been embarrassing for him, Peter came knowing that both he and Jesus knew about the past and the present, the sin and the shame. Jesus asked "do you love me" because he wanted Peter to be **free** from the guilt and shame, the self-protection and hiding behind a façade. Jesus wanted him to admit his failure, yes, but admit it in light of the cross and resurrection, and the new freedom and identity that brings.

Slide 7 – Personal Testimony

What identity, what names have you been carrying around with you?
We need to come before God and be willing to say, "My name is..."
Pervert, glutton, unworthy, impatient, drunkard, coward, unattractive, liar, drug addict, "mommy porn" addict, lazy, cheater, adulterer? My name is betrayer, abuser, thief, murderer, greed, selfish, rebellion, homosexual, rage, envy, stubborn. My name is unlovable, manipulator, fearful, self-hater, incompetent, worthless, failure, fake. My name is deceiver, bitter, lust, revenge, fornicator, oppressor.

Whew: that's a lot of yuck, isn't it? But listen, we need to be willing to say, "This is who I am... God, change me."

Jesus wants to set you free from all those false names and identities this weekend. But you must confess them to Him, you must bring them into the light and come real so that you can be free from the secrets that you think disqualify you and drive you to isolate. Jesus has a new name for you that He wants you to receive. He wants you to share in his inheritance as a daughter.

There is no reason for you to leave this retreat disappointed with God. Look any and all insecurity in the face and declare that you are here to *Encounter God*. He promises He is near to all of us who are ready to seek Him from the deep places of longing in our hearts.

This weekend we will **identify** the things in our past and present that are blocks to receiving God's perfect love, and we will **turn** from them. We will **break** the power of them over our lives, **release** our burdens to Jesus, and will **receive** His love, peace, and healing presence in those places. Jesus is bubbling over with joy at the thought of doing this with you.

Slide 8 – The 4 Rs

We've got a tool for you to use this weekend that we like to call **The 4 R's**, and if you have a pen, please find a place in your booklet to write these down.

1. Repent

2. Renounce

3. Release

4. Receive

Think of this as a picture of a very favorite jacket that you've had for years – it's worn out and not pretty, but it's so familiar and comfortable that you wear it all the time without hardly ever bothering to take it off. It's full of holes and you rarely bother to wash it, so it probably stinks—but hey, it's super comfy. Putting it on is such a habit that you don't have to think about it, and it feels like it fits perfectly. Think of your sin as this old jacket. It's ugly but it feels like it belongs on you.

When using the 4 Rs, **Repent** is to decide to <u>agree with God about your sin</u> (*write that down!*), that it's nasty. **Renounce** is to <u>decide to take it off, that you don't want it anymore</u>. **Release** is to not just decide to throw it away, but <u>to give</u>

it to Jesus at the cross. **Receive** is to then put on the spirit of Jesus in those heart places, put on the beautiful new outfit that Jesus has for you in place of the old.

We will be talking about the 4 Rs a lot more this weekend and whenever you come for prayer ministry, we will lead you in a prayer along these lines.

- Come expecting—and leave with a new identity

- Come hungry—and leave satisfied

- Come alone—and leave with a new relationship with God

- Come willing to be broken—and leave healed

- Come real—and leave with a new reality

Sin: The Way of Death

Slide 1 – The Garden

In the beginning, God created all—plants, animals, the sky, the sea, the stars and moon, and planets—and called them *good*. Then He formed man and woman and placed them in a garden and called them very *very good*. They were called *very good* not because they were just another creature to fill the earth, but because they were created as the Image of God, to stand for Creation to God as priests, to stand for God to Creation as prophets, and to rule with divinely appointed authority over all the earth. They were given all things but were charged with one rule: not to eat of the Tree of the Knowledge of Good and Evil. This meant they were to live in a loving, trust-based relationship with God, freely chosen by obedience.

But the serpent came with lies. Lies lead to doubt, doubt of God's goodness and love, and doubt leads to fear, fear that we will not have enough and not be protected or satisfied, and fear leads to raising ourselves up as the standard of truth. Our first parents did this. They chose to set themselves up as gods instead of trusting that the God who created them and provided for them would continue to give them what they needed. And instantly, the Image of God in them was broken. They no longer trusted God, and they could no longer trust each other. They were ashamed in their nakedness, and they hid. They ran *from* God instead of *to* Him with their failure and their shame, and when God sought them out, they blamed each other and the serpent instead of confessing their own sin. Pride and self replaced humility and God.

We continue this same cycle in our own lives: we believe the lies; we set up "self" as an idol; we hide in shame and continue to pass the blame.

Slide 2 – The Law

Once people no longer lived forever, self-preservation became central to their existence. God gave the law to teach, train, and preserve community.

Without it, our bent is toward self-preservation at any cost. Through the law, God required that all intentional sin be cut off to preserve holiness, so people wouldn't become completely hardened to cooperating with God's grace in their lives. God established the sacrificial system for unintentional sin and for disease. But there were no sacrifices sufficient for intentional sin. The only consequence for intentional sin was death.

God's law is ABSOLUTE because God is absolutely holy, and only those who are holy can engage in relationship with Him.

Slide 3 – Jesus

Jesus took up the themes of sin, obedience, and love during his earthly ministry. He instructed his followers that sin needs to be cut off. He taught that those who desire relationship with God still need to engage in trust-based obedience by choosing to trust what God says about good and evil and ruthlessly deal with sin in their lives.

Slide 4 – Paul

Paul describes how, apart from Christ, we are controlled by sin. We are not even free to love and obey God when we are slaves to sin.

Slide 5 – Sin's New Names

- Sin is not a popular term, even among Christians. In fact, if you were to walk up to almost anyone and say, "You are a sinner," you would probably elicit a reaction that would be unfavorable to your body.

- So, we use more comfortable names for sin: faults, shortcomings, hang-ups, problems, issues, mistakes, dysfunction, slip ups, things we fall into.

- We call sin by these other names so that we can avoid thinking about the truth that we have broken God's laws, that we answer to him, and that we are responsible for our own actions.

- However, the reality is that SIN is SIN, and we all sin many times a day. If we commit just one sin a day every day, in the average life, we would commit over 30,000 sins. If you were being tried in a court of law with a record of 30,000 repeat offenses, and you were guilty of all of them, you would be in more than just a little bit of trouble.

- Jesus spoke seriously about sin and the need to understand what effect it has on us and those around us.

6. What Is Sin?

- The most common use of the word sin in the New Testament is pronounced "ha-mart-tee-a" (*hamartia*)... meaning, "to miss the mark." "For all have sinned and fall short of the glory of God" (Romans 3:23).

- Sin as a singular act is a symptom of being a sinner. Hamartia refers to an ongoing condition and is used 55 times in Paul's letters.

- What "mark" is it that we are missing? When God's Word says that all fall short of the glory of God, that means that no one can compare to God's infinite holiness and moral purity. God's unapproachable light and holiness will not tolerate darkness and wickedness. Even the slightest deviation from absolute perfection cannot abide in His presence. In order to enjoy fellowship with God, one must be blameless in holiness before him, sharing in the quality of His glory. The mark, or standard for relationship and entrance into heaven, is absolute perfection, blamelessness, and spotlessness. It is to be glorious like God.

- What is God's glory? It is not God's perfection; it is not God's holiness. God's glory is man fully alive. God's glory is men and women living as the unbroken images of God. God did not give us an unattainable goal. He did not say "I am God, and if you are not like Me, you fall short." We cannot fall short of what we were not created to be. We were created to be the image of God: to represent Him to the world, to represent the world to Him, and to be seated in authority.

- The world measures perfection based on intelligence, education, financial success, political power, and religious performance.

- But God does not acknowledge these standards; His standard is Himself and His own glory, and it is impossible for God to deviate from that or tolerate anything less. If He did, He'd cease to be holy, and He'd cease to be God.

Slide 7 – Types of Sin

All sin falls into these three categories:

- **Transgression (Commission)**: Willfully doing what God forbids. "For whoever shall keep the whole law, and yet stumble in one point, he is guilty of all" (James 2:10). For example: seeing a "NO trespassing" sign and trespassing anyway.

- **Omission:** A failure to do the will of God. "Therefore, to him who knows to do good and does not do it, to him it is sin" (James 4:17). For example: the parable of the Good Samaritan—ignoring those in need.

- **Self-Exaltation:** A lack of desire to do God's will or doing God's will for ungodly reasons. For example: agreeing to obey but with a bad attitude or with the sole desire for self-advancement.

  "Not everyone who says to Me, 'Lord, Lord,' shall enter the kingdom of heaven, but he who does the will of My Father in heaven. Many will say to Me in that day, 'Lord, Lord, have we not prophesied in Your name, cast out demons in Your name, and done many wonders in Your name?' And then I will declare to them, 'I never knew you; depart from Me, you who practice lawlessness!'" (Matt. 7:21–23)

Slide 8 – Effects of Sin

Sin makes humanity an enemy of God: "And you, who once were alienated and enemies in your mind by wicked works..." (Colossians 1:21)

- It alienates us from God because of shame.

- It makes us offended at God.

- It makes us haters of God.

- It makes us dull and resistant to God.

- It deprives us of relationship with God.

- It deprives us of our human potential in God.

- Sin corrupts our desires: We become slaves to things that do not actually benefit us, including addictions like food, drugs, alcohol, pornography, approval, success.

- Sin attacks our bodies: We know from science that stress, hatred, gluttony, and sexual promiscuity can have negative effects on our bodies.

- Sin steals our rest and peace: Sin keeps us up at night! We expend a lot of energy to figure out ways to keep it secret and cope with the shame of it. It makes silence scary, and so we look for things to medicate the inner turmoil.

- Sin distorts our consciences: Sin in our lives makes it impossible to discern reality—what is really true, what is actually happening. Psalm 115 says those who worship idols (who have replaced the one true God in their hearts with something else) will be like those idols, having no real ability to see, hear, smell, feel, etc.

- Sin alters our appearance: Sin ages us and harms our physical appearance.

- Sin degrades our minds: We experience vain imagination, depression, obsessive thoughts, anxiety, etc.

- And sin destroys our eternal destiny: Our destiny is to reign with Christ, to be kings, priests and co-regents, but sin will take all of that away.

- Sin destroys our friendship and intimacy with God and hinders our prayers.

- On our end: We were created to enjoy God, but sin will cause us to struggle to even know Him or hear His voice.

- On God's end: The Lord will often remain uncomfortably silent if we stubbornly persist in sin.

  But your iniquities have separated you from your God; and your sins have hidden His face from you, so that He will not hear. (Isaiah 59:2)

- Instead of enjoying God, we struggle with intimacy, worship and prayer.

Slide 9 – Who Sin Affects

The *state* of sin is what we are born into. It is our birthright. It is the broken Image of God in us. The *act* of sin is what we choose to do that breaks that Image further in us and others.

- Sin will affect us personally, depriving us of the joy, pleasure, and peace God has promised those who abide in him. Sin affects our offspring. It introduces hurt, insecurity, and various generational cycles of sin for years to come.

  You shall not worship them or serve them for I, the Lord your God, am a jealous God, visiting the iniquity of the fathers on the children, and on the third and fourth generations of those who hate me." (Deut. 5:9–10)

- Sin affects the Body of Christ.

> *And if one member suffers, all the members suffer with it; or if one member is honored, all the members rejoice with it. (1 Cor. 12:26)*

- We are not a single unit but a part of something that is so much greater than ourselves. Sin defiles the Bride of Christ of which we are a part: it distorts her beauty in the world and erects barriers to healthy and transparent relationships in the church.

- The modern lie is that our sin is personal and has no effect on the rest of the body. We often hear people say, "Well, as long as I'm not hurting anybody else, it isn't actually bad." But our sin will often cause us to isolate ourselves, alienate others, and allow relationships to deteriorate.

We keep talking about sin in light of what we have done, but there are also sins done against us that keep us bound and broken, such as deep wounds of mind and soul, unforgiveness and bitterness.

Slide 10 – Our Partnership With Sin

There are many ways that we partner with sin:

- Unbelief/Unforgiveness: It's important to understand that forgiveness is giving up our right to retribution. It does not make sins against us "okay." When we forgive, we simply release the right to judge and leave the retribution to God. When there has been sin, there needs to be forgiveness, whether we feel hurt or not. Unforgiveness is like drinking poison and waiting for the other person to die. A root of bitterness: being bitter toward others, critical, cynical, judgmental. Having difficulty with other's weaknesses, and difficulty forgiving. Sexual Perversion/FantasyPrideFear

- Greed/Jealousy/Apathy: Indifference and laziness concerning our lives in God and our commitment to follow Jesus.

Include your testimony here:

- What have you been set free from? *Name the sin.*

- How did the sin impact your life? Relationships? Prayer? *Be specific.*

- Who was hurt by your sin? What happened?

- How did you come to realize it was sin?

- What did God do for you? How are you changed?

Slide 11 – Sin Ends in Death

Sin ends in death for those who do not repent and who continue to partner with sin, because the cross is only for those who want to be free. God has made the provision, but we must appropriate it.

For the wages of sin is death. (Romans 6:23)

When a righteous man turns away from his righteousness, commits iniquity, and dies in it, it is because of the iniquity which he has done that he dies. (Ezekiel 18:26)

We often make excuses for our sins:

- "I am not really that bad. The things I do aren't that terrible."

- "Well, I'm not hurting anyone."

- "I have other things to deal with; I don't have time for that now."

- "I have come a long way; I'll get to that soon."

- "God loves me. He knows I'm weak, so He'll forgive me anyway."

These excuses make it sound as if some sin is acceptable, as if some sins can be considered non-destructive. The truth is that God does not give us the latitude to commit *any* sin. In God's eyes, all sin equally falls short of his infinite glory.

When we fail to acknowledge and repent of sin in our lives, thus beginning a new lifestyle of repentance, we are not cooperating with the grace of God in our lives, and we are setting ourselves up to commit many sins. The effects of sins are cumulative.

A sinful pattern that is allowed to remain will affect our consciences and allow additional sins to be committed to the point where we lose any ability to live an abundant life. Sin is like cancer unchecked. In the end it will choke out all life and kill us.

The final excuse for sin is often this: "I am just too weak to resist sin."

That excuse is without merit. God has given each of us a way out, a way to be free from sin's devastating effects, and a way to turn from sin wherever and whenever we find it. **That way** is what the next session is all about.

The Cross

Slide 1 – The Cross

Slide 2 – In the Beginning

We live in a broken world. But in the beginning, God created everything, and it was *good*. Adam and Eve were the original image bearers of God: they walked in His authority, ruling over and caring for Creation, and they enjoyed true intimacy with God. But they chose to forfeit all of that. Instead of trusting God and His goodness and love, they went their own way, bringing bitterness and destruction into their hearts and lives.And we have all tasted the sting of that moment. Our own disobedience has borne the fruit of alienation and isolation from God as a direct reflection of that moment. Feelings of shame, guilt, hopelessness: these are all a continuation of Adam and Eve's story being played out in our own lives. It's the curse, the sickness of sin.

But God knew Adam and Eve would mistrust Him. He knew we too would eat the forbidden fruit. And He had a rescue plan from the foundations of the world. Redemption was in the heart of God before time began, and from the time of Adam, our God began to unfold His amazing plan.

Slide 3 – What Is the Plan?

After God's relationship with man was broken, God comes to an idol worshipper named Abram to reinitiate relationship—not because Abram was good, but because God *Himself* is good. God loves sinners. He calls them out and saves them. He rescues His enemies. God told Abram, "Go to the land I will show you." He didn't tell Abram where he was going. He told Abram, "I'll show you when you get there." And then **God makes Abram an incredible promise**: That he would be the father of many nations. He would have descendants outnumbering the stars in heaven and the grains of sand and through Abram's offspring, God would bless the whole Earth.

Slide 4 – Cutting a Covenant

Then, in Genesis 15, God seals his covenant with Abram in the same way that kings at that time would seal a sacred treaty.

In the Ancient Near East, a greater king would make promises of protection to a lesser king, who would promise loyalty. The greater leader would confer, by grace, the capacity to come into relationship. They would seal the treaty not by signing a paper but by "cutting the covenant." They would slaughter animals and cut them in half, signifying that the two kings' lives are joined together. Then they would arrange them so that there was a bloody pathway between the pieces, and the two kings would walk through them saying, "If I break this covenant with you, may it be done to me as has been done to these animals."

So, when God told Abram to go get the animals, Abram knew exactly what was going on. He cut the animals in half, arranged them, and waited. Then, Abram became overwhelmed with the presence of God, and saw God, who was manifesting Himself as a flaming firepot, walk between the pieces alone. He did not ask Abram to walk with Him. He sealed the covenant with Abram, walking through the blood, signifying that if the covenant relationship was broken, he would be the one to die.

In this covenant, God and Abram become joined together. Later, God gives Abram and Sarai a piece of His own identity by giving them part of His name. From YHWH, Abram would become Abraham and Sarai would become Sarah. God did this knowing full well that Abram and his descendants could not keep covenant with Him. The Bible tells the story of a people who, like Adam before them, and all of us after them, fail to fully trust and obey God.

And so, as promised, God has exacted the consequences of all of this—not from us, though we deserve it, but from Himself. And, to do that, He became one of us, flesh and blood.

Slide 5 – Jesus

With no reluctance in His heart, Jesus Christ, who was 100% God and 100% man, became like those animals in the ritual. He took upon Himself once and for all the punishment for broken covenant. The blood of animals cannot pay for human sin: there must be an equivalent sacrifice. The price for your sin and my sin was paid for by the perfect God-man. Jesus didn't die so much "for you" as He died "as you" upon the cross. You have nothing to do with saving yourself. You can't afford the price and continue living. Jesus bore your penalty in your stead. You have been called out, made clean, and given a promise. Not because you are good, but because He is good.

In order to receive this, you must believe it. You must trust that God is who He said He is and that He's done what He promised. We must believe that we are actually broken, and that there is nothing we can do to earn our freedom, AND we must believe that our freedom from guilt and the victory over sin was actually won for us at the cross. Therefore, where we deserve judgment, we will instead find mercy, grace, and love beyond anything we would dare to hope for.

Slide 6 – The Cross

The mercy that I received and continue to receive is something I cannot turn my back on because it was given to me at a very high cost. Jesus in the Garden the night before He was arrested, was faced with the reality that He was going to have to die a brutal death, become sin for our sake, and be separated from the Father for the first time in all of eternity!

He knew the plan was the only way & still tried to escape it!

But there was no other way because the wage of sin is death. The cost of my sin and your sin is death. He willingly paid that price for you by being brutally murdered, crucified, and separated from God.

We did this. We deserved this. I deserved this. But because of the cross, I received mercy instead.

Slide 7 – Identification: The Will

At Gethsemane, Christ identified with us when He prayed "not my will but yours" (Matt 26:39). Going a little farther, He fell with His face to the ground and prayed, "My Father, if it is possible, may this cup be taken from me. Yet not as I will, but as you will."

We are no longer slaves. We can no longer say that we are enslaved by our will. Jesus has made a way for us to have a will fully committed to God. Where Adam said "No," Jesus said "Yes." Where your sin nature said "No," the new creation says "Yes."

Adam did what he wanted rather than what God commanded, which is the sin of rebellion. When Jesus sweat drops of blood as He faced the trial of the cross and said, "Father, Your will and not My will be done," He won the victory over our will. We have the power through Christ to choose what is right. No longer can we say "Yes, this is why I react in sinful ways because of my personality (my parents, my past, or the other person)... *blah blah blah.*"

If we are in Christ, then we are not slaves to sin. We can say "Yes" to God. It is a choice we can make.

Slide 8 – Identification: Shame

Christ identified with our shame and humiliation as a result of sin.

Confessing sin and coming clean can feel humiliating. True conviction is from God to lead us to repentance, but shame is from Satan. True guilt has to do with what you've done, but shame has to do with who you are. We can often tell the difference between guilt and shame after we have repented of sin because shame tends to keep convincing us that we are defiled, dirty, and unworthy. We feel condemned and like hopeless hypocrites. By bearing the shame—the mockery of the crown of thorns, as well as His nakedness and the utter curse that it was to be nailed to a tree—Jesus identified with the shame and humiliation sin brings, nailing it to the cross.

He has broken the power of shame. When you renounce it in His name, it is removed. By the power of the cross, you *can* walk without shame.

Slide 9 – Identification: Healing

We need to believe that Jesus took our punishment and that **his wounds** mean **our healing**. The word "salvation" is also translated "healing" and points to the full restoration of the whole person in the image of God.

> Surely he took up our pain
> and bore our suffering,
> yet we considered him punished by God,

stricken by him, and afflicted.
But he was pierced for our transgressions,
  he was crushed for our iniquities;
the punishment that brought us peace was on him,
  and by his wounds we are healed.
We all, like sheep, have gone astray,
  each of us has turned to our own way;
and the Lord has laid on him
  the iniquity of us all. (Isa. 53:4–6)

Slide 10 – Identification: Sacrifice

Christ is the one who paid the **ultimate sacrifice on the cross** for our sin.

In Philippians 2, St. Paul says that "Christ was obedient to death, even the death on the cross." This was the most horrible death that was known to humanity. After Jesus' crucifixion, the Romans had to stop using it because it became a symbol of such honor. God paid the price of sin and as the last Adam, gave us back the power and authority that Adam and Eve abdicated so that we can take dominion over the sin that so easily entangles us.

Because of Christ's sacrifice on the cross, the promise of restoration is fulfilled, and the covenant is upheld in all its love and glory.

Slide 11 – Testimony

Include your testimony here:

- What have you been set free from? *Name the sin.*

- How did the sin impact your life? Relationships? Prayer? *Be specific.*

- Who was hurt by your sin? What happened?

- How did you come to realize it was sin?

- What did God do for you? How are you changed?

Slide 12 – How Do We Receive It?

The posture for receiving this freedom, healing and salvation is **humility**.

Some of us Christians walk through life confessing that we are saved by grace through faith and do not believe that we have a need to confess sin because, after all, "His grace is sufficient." But the fact is that becoming a Christian is only the beginning of a lifelong process whereby the image of God is restored in us. We need to be saved daily and continually renewed and empowered by the Holy Spirit.

In order for this to happen, we must agree with God's way of seeing things, we must agree with His evaluation of our lives, and when we come up short, we must acknowledge it and confess it. The Bible says, "When we **confess** our sin He is faithful and just to forgive our sin and cleanse us from all unrighteousness."If we rename sin and call it something different (paint a new reality), then we feel as if we have nothing to confess because it's no big deal, and we cannot receive the freedom of being saved. Jesus modeled humility when He, the God-man, left Heaven, was born into a feeding trough, became like us in every way yet was without sin, and suffered at the hands of the men He created. He was stripped naked and beaten by his own creation. The judge became the judged. He humbled Himself, saving no dignity or reputation, and died on a cross. If God humbled Himself for our benefit, how can we expect to receive freedom without the same humility? If God gave up His whole reputation, why do we expect to save ours? We must humble ourselves, agree with his evaluation of our lives and confess our sin before Him.

The requirement here is complete honesty, complete humility. You must bring who you are to the cross and to your sisters or brothers around you. Become a **transparent** man/woman with nothing to hide. Our sin doesn't surprise God; it hasn't caught Him off guard. We can come out of the shadows, step into the light, and stop hiding, because we are safe and hidden deep in the heart of God. If you are already saved, you are washed clean by His blood, and now He longs to wash your conscience so you can see yourself the way He sees you. If you have not yet yielded yourself to Jesus, you must humble yourself by stripping yourself of a desire to save your own reputation, agree with His evaluation of your life, confess your sins and receive the grace of God through faith.

Slide 13 – Beyond the Cross

God has not set us free to live in the shadow of shame, constantly reminded of our sin and shortcomings, to suffer the effects of dysfunctional structures in our lives. Not an ounce, not a second of shame is appropriate in the believer's life. Jesus has set us free to be free indeed. Jesus not only bore the *punishment* of our sin, by dying *as us* on the cross, he also broke the *power* of sin in our lives. God has called us to live in freedom now, fully confident that His blood was enough, enjoy unhindered relationship with Him, and the overwhelming joy of living in the power of the Holy Spirit.

>>>PASSION CLIP<<<

Healing Our Image of God

Slide 1 – Healing Our Image of God:

Goal of talk—To introduce the idea that our image of God matters, is influenced largely by our father, mother, and other key authority figures (particularly from childhood), can be both wounded and healed, and results in our understanding of who we are, who God is, and how He feels and acts toward us.

Slide 2 – In the Beginning... Broken

In the beginning, the accuser, Satan, sought to drive a wedge between the Creator and the created by insinuating that God did not have the best interests of the newly formed Image Bearers at heart.

> *The serpent was clever, more clever than any wild animal God had made. He spoke to the Woman: "Do I understand that God told you not to eat from any tree in the garden?" The Woman said to the serpent, "Not at all. We can eat from the trees in the garden. It's only about the tree in the middle of the garden that God said, 'Don't eat from it; don't even touch it or you'll die.'" The serpent told the Woman, "You won't die. God knows that the moment you eat from that tree, you'll see what's really going on. You'll be just like God, knowing everything, ranging all the way from good to evil."* (Genesis 3, MSG)

Slide 3 – I Was Afraid, Because I Was Naked

When the woman saw that the tree looked like good eating and realized what she would get out of it—she'd know everything!—she took and ate the fruit and then gave some to her husband, and he ate. Immediately the two of them did "see what's really going on"—and they saw themselves naked! They sewed fig leaves together as makeshift clothes for themselves. When they heard the sound of God strolling in the garden in the evening breeze, the man and his wife hid from God in the trees of the garden. God called to the man: "Where are you?" He said, "I heard you in the garden and I was afraid because I was naked. And I hid."

The immediate result of eating the forbidden fruit was shame and unhealthy fear of God. Eve believed a lie about God: that His heart toward her was not for her growth, success, and happiness, and the lie formed a foundation for disobedience, resulting in shame and separation from God.

Slide 4 – Image Matters

Our image of God matters. A.W. Tozer writes in his book *The Knowledge of the Holy*, that "What comes into our minds when we think about God is the most important thing about us." It matters how we perceive what God is like, how he acts, and how He feels about us. These images color the way we pray, the way we read the Bible, and the way we interact with those around us. If I feel loved by God, it is possible for me to extend that love to others. If I feel judged (even though I am pardoned through the sacrifice of Jesus Christ), I will judge myself and others. If I feel ashamed before God, I will be more likely to do that which is shameful. If I feel unworthy before God, I will be more likely to get my sense of self-worth from what I do or fail to do, the people who love me or hate me, the money or power I have or I don't.

Francis MacNutt writes: "We must distinguish between knowing God and simply believing in him. Knowing God on a personal, intimate level goes beyond an intellectual 'head' knowledge of him, such as we gain through studying Scripture. Yet many Christians do not really know God on an intimate, personal level" (Francis MacNutt, *School of Healing Prayer, Level 1 Manual*, 55). It is often a distorted view of God that prevents us from pursuing and achieving true intimacy with God.

Slide 5 – The Camera Sometimes Lies

Often the pictures of God we have in our minds are ones of a distant, angry, passive, or retributive God. Some common lies include, "I am unworthy of

God's love," "It is God's will for me to suffer," "God may be love, but His love is so different than mine that it is completely unrecognizable as love," and "I have to work to earn God's approval." But those pictures are not born in a vacuum. They come from somewhere. We're going to look at three sources for these broken images of God, and then at what it means to have these images healed.

Slide 6 – All Are Broken

All men are broken, and broken men break their children who grow up to be broken men… (Misty Edwards, *All Men are Broken*)

Our earthly parents were created to show us what God looks like, as earthly representations of His image…When we look at them, we see through them, as through a window… and that is the view of God we have. If they are cracked and broken, that is the view of God that we have.

Slide 7 – The Father Wound

At the very core of every human being is the cry for fatherhood. We are like heat-seeking missiles searching for the heat of a dad's love. Without it, we are misguided, aimlessly destroying everything in our path until we find it.

It is not enough for a father to provide shelter, food and clothing. It is not even enough for a father to have feelings for his children. Those feelings must be communicated and expressed in a way that is meaningful to each child. Sons and daughters need to feel safe both physically and emotionally. Kids need to know they have a safe place in their father's hearts, no matter how much they fail. Witnessing explosive anger and rage is frightening for children. They need an atmosphere of unconditional love and acceptance. While even adults want other people to say good things about them, children especially need this from their fathers, and many spend their lives trying to gain the approval of their father. Dr. Dobson said, "It takes 40 words of praise to counteract just one word of criticism in a child's heart."

God the Father said to Jesus, "You are my beloved Son, in whom I am well pleased." Earthly fathers are responsible to provide:

- Meaningful touch

- Loving shelter: discipline & safety

- Words of life

- Valued as a son or daughter with unconditional love

- A prophetic destiny: point us to the father and our purpose

- An active commitment to our success

Children look to their fathers to meet these emotional and physical needs, but unfortunately, no earthly father is perfect. At some point, disappointments, hurts and wounds will inevitably take place and cause "father wounds" to form in the hearts of children.

The leftover pain and wounds from childhood can create a lens through which adults later view the world and God.

Slide 8 – Who's Your Daddy?

No earthly father is perfect. Because of our brokenness, disappointments and hurts will take place, and when they do, they cause wounds to form in our hearts. The leftover pain and wounds from childhood create a lens through which we view the world and God, a distorted view of God. Most of the time we have a warped way of perceiving and relating to God because of the way we were brought up. We make judgments because of the way we experienced our own fathers. Even the word "Father" makes some people cringe due to difficult relationships experienced with earthly fathers. Unfortunately, these relationships can keep us from finding intimacy with God, the true Father.

- **Good father:** Though imperfect, a good father is stable, loving, affirming, and consistently provides for needs.

- **Performance-oriented father:** Expresses love when you have measured up to rigid expectations; has stringent demands for perfect obedience and high performance standards; often uses guilt and shame to maintain control.

- **Authoritarian father:** Demands immediate, unquestioned obedience; uses intimidation and fear to maintain control; tends to be very selfish: the entire life of a family often revolves around them.

- **Passive father:** Makes no great demands or even often overtly rejects children; fails to be "home" even when he is home; unable to demonstrate any sort of love or affection (usually because he did not receive as a child); doesn't share his feelings; just "lives" under the same roof as family.

- **Absentee father:** No longer physically or emotionally present in the home, either through death, divorce, or abandonment.

- **Abusive father:** Is emotionally, verbally, physically, and/or sexually abusive.

Slide 9 – The Wound's Effect

How does this affect our daily lives? What do we look like?

1. **Addictions**

   a) use of drugs/alcohol to numb the pain

   b) sexual addiction to fill the need

   c) false intimacy (IN-TO-ME-SEE), poor marriage and other relationships

2. **Driven**

   a) workaholic

   b) people pleaser

   c) ulcers, headaches, stress, anger

   d) fear of life and failure

   e) depression

3. **Passive**

a) no motivation for life—unhappy in job, ministry, marriage

b) quitter

c) angry, but hold it in

d) chronic illness

e) low self-esteem

f) emotions are kept on the back burner (buried, waiting to come out in another way)

g) rebellion

4. **Poverty Mentality**

a) It never feels like there is enough for you (you become greedy and hoard)

b) You always struggle with money, which leads to strife in the home

c) Orphan heart instead of a heart of sonship

d) Causes us to resist Jesus leading us to the Father

Slide 10 – The Mother Wound

A mother's love lays the foundation of love, emotion, and sense of self. The influence of a mother starts at conception, so wounds can begin early.

Beyond basic physical survival needs, infants have need for affectionate touch, eye contact and loving words. Deprivation in these areas can cause significant physical and emotional brokenness. Wounding can be the result of sickness of the mother or child, death, divorce, or separation. Other childhood traumas that can be the cause of a mother wound can derive from instances such as neglect, abuse, the mother's mental/emotional distress, attempted abortion, or the immaturity of a teenage/young mother.

Slide 11 – Are You My Mother?

The mother wound causes the following issues:

- difficulties for a person to connect with others in a deep way; an inability to communicate well; not being able to say what you mean to say; an inability to give and receive affection;

- feelings of abandonment and dread of aloneness;

- feeling a loss of self and being;

- having powerful hunger for feminine touch that can be eroticized;

- unhealthy emotional dependency on others;

- possible gender confusion;

- fear and insecurity; internalizing a poor view of women;

- having addictive, emotional and romantic dependencies.

Not all these symptoms are caused by a mother wound, but many are often associated.

Slide 12 – Church and Spiritual Authority Wounds

Much can be said about the influence of the Christian Church, and spiritual authorities, on our understanding of who God is and what He is like. We must be intentional about who we allow to teach us about God. What is communicated about God by these sources can be separated into two categories: 1) what is taught about God, and 2) how those in the church did, or did not, walk out that teaching.

Slide 13 – Out of Sync

Jesus had his harshest teaching directed at the teachers of the law who had studied the scriptures but were devoid of relationship with the living God, and so could not perceive or understand God's nature, or his self-revelation through Jesus Christ. John 5:39–41 reads:

> *You search the Scriptures because you think that in them you have eternal life; and it is they that bear witness about me, yet you refuse to come to me that you may have life. I do*

not receive glory from people. But I know that you do not have the love of God within you.

Jesus brought a message of repentance, reconciliation with the Father, and the destruction of the works of the devil through His Earthly ministry, the continuation of the advancing Kingdom of Heaven through His followers, and eventually and completely with His second coming.

When the Church is out of sync with the heart of God in these matters, spiritual abuse often occurs. Teaching can fall short because of its limited scope (through neglecting essential truths about life in the Kingdom of God) or downright error.

Spiritual abuse can manifest as law-based conformity that replaces intimacy and power through the Holy Spirit with "being right," or lawlessness that uses a false teaching about grace to justify sinful actions and mindsets. Both abuses boil down to our "rightful spiritual freedom [being] taken away by people we regard as spiritual authorities," as opposed to listening to the Holy Spirit and following His guidance.

Slide 14 – Do as I Say, Not as I Do

God has entrusted profound spiritual influence to the Church and her teachers. What we experience in church often plays a significant role in establishing our image of God. The image of God is quickly distorted in an environment of rampant hypocrisy, or teaching one thing and acting out another. The manifestations of this can range from teaching about love but the acting out of judgment, acknowledging the Trinity but denying, neglecting, or even forbidding the present-day ministry of the Holy Spirit as revealed in the scriptures, all the way to verbal, physical, emotional, and even sexual abuse within the church. Hypocrisy results in profound destruction of a healthy image of God. Because God has chosen to reveal Himself through the Church, when the church (particularly, a church leader) claims to represent God but instead acts carnally, those affected often reject the church altogether, becoming unwilling or even unable to take their place in a healthy Church community.

Slide 15 – Journey of Healing

How can we be healed from all these wounds? If we do not know Jesus, we can never satisfy this cry. Jesus is the only way to the Father. This is where our healing begins. We can...

- Develop a relationship with the Father, Son, and Holy Spirit

- Begin with forgiveness

- Step courageously from shame into freedom

Slide 16 – Healing Flows

We can know that:

- Healing is a journey, and we cannot heal ourselves

- Healing flows from intimacy with God

- Healing flows from authentic imagery of God

- Healing flows from healthy intimacy with people

Slide 17 – "They will know me"

"That's right. The time is coming when I will make a brand-new covenant with Israel and Judah. It won't be a repeat of the covenant I made with their ancestors when I took their hand to lead them out of the land of Egypt. They broke that covenant even though I did my part as their Master." God's Decree. "This is the brand-new covenant that I will make with Israel when the time comes. I will put my law within them—write it on their hearts! —and be their God. And they will be my people. They will no longer go around setting up schools to teach each other about God. They'll know me firsthand, the dull and the bright, the smart and the slow. I'll wipe the slate clean for each of them. I'll forget they ever sinned!" God's Decree. (Jeremiah 31:31–34 MSG)

The promise God made in Jeremiah was that a time was coming when everybody could know God and know what he was like. The beginning of healing our image of God is belief that through the Holy Spirit, we can grow in right knowledge of who God is and how He feels about us.

Include your testimony here:

- How was your view of the image of God broken?

- How did this impact your life? Relationships? Prayer? Your own sin? *Be specific.*

- Who was hurt by this? What happened?

- How did you come to realize that your view of God was distorted?

- What did God do for you? How were you healed?

Sexual Wholeness: Telling God's Story

Slide 1 – Introduction

Slide 2 – John 8:1–11

...Jesus went to the Mount of Olives.

At dawn he appeared again in the temple courts, where all the people gathered around him, and he sat down to teach them. The teachers of the law and the Pharisees brought in a woman caught in adultery. They made her stand before the group and said to Jesus, "Teacher, this woman was caught in the act of adultery. In the Law Moses commanded us to stone such women. Now what do you say?" They were using this question as a trap, in order to have a basis for accusing him.

But Jesus bent down and started to write on the ground with his finger. When they kept on questioning him, he straightened up and said to them, "Let any one of you who is without sin be the first to throw a stone at her." Again he stooped down and wrote on the ground.

At this, those who heard began to go away one at a time, the older ones first, until only Jesus was left, with the woman still standing there. Jesus straightened up and asked her, "Woman, where are they? Has no one condemned you?"

"No one, sir," she said.

"Then neither do I condemn you," Jesus declared. "Go now and leave your life of sin."

The first thing we need to establish when beginning a session on human sexuality is that conversations surrounding human sexuality are *as charged as they are* precisely because sexuality is one of *the most charged aspects of being a human.* If you think in terms of energy output and the ability to generate power, sex has so much power it has the potential to make more humans. Throughout the history of the world, conversations, restrictions, laws, misdeeds, poetry, wounds, healing and pain have swirled around sexuality, precisely because it has so much power and so much potential for goodness and for pain. And it makes sense that something that has the power to generate humans equally contains the power to destroy them. But it wasn't meant to be this way.

Slide 3 – Where Does the Pain Come From?

Slide 4 – The World Has Failed Us

i. Obsession and reductionism: Sex is everything, and sex is nothing. *I am* my sexuality, who or what I am sexually attracted to, or how I have been mistreated or abused, but the act of sex or sexual activities have little or no significance beyond mutual consent. You can have sex whenever, however, and with whomever you want, as there are believed to be no long-term effects, no real consequences, no real meaning or significance.

ii. Hypersexualized marketing: If there's one thing that is evident in today's commercial sector, it is that sex sells. Sex and sexiness drive up profits for items otherwise unrelated to sex, and the pornography industry is estimated to generate an annual revenue of $90 billion as of 2019. On demand pornography is producing a generation of men and women whose sexuality is completely devoid of human connection. Something that's meant to lead to intimacy is either less intimate than sharing your phone number (hookup culture) or doesn't even involve another human (porn, technosex, etc.). We've reduced sex to scratching an itch, mechanically meeting a biological urge in the least human way possible.

iii. The sexual revolution of the 1960s encouraged us to follow whatever desires we have, guaranteed that if we do not deny our desires, we will certainly arrive at ultimate satisfaction. ***If it feels good,*** it is good for you. So if it feels good, do it! This is also reflected in our healthcare and therapeutic systems, which have shifted their goals from "wellness" (measurable by scientific standards), to "well being" (defined by personal satisfaction), to embrace the freedom to follow desires, rather than be limited by traditional or even scientifically verifiable definitions of wellness. This obsession may lead to short-term enjoyment and satisfaction. But, like junk food, it will usually leave us feeling overindulged, lethargic, less powerful, and not satisfied at the deepest levels in the long run.

Slide 5 – The Church Has Often Failed Us

i. Silence and negativity: **Silence,** because we often lack a God-sized understanding of sexuality. We don't know how the gospel (the good news!) matters to sexuality, other than putting limits on sexual expression. And **negativity** is rooted in a heresy that goes back to the first century and has permeated the church since the beginning.

ii. Gnosticism: An age-old heresy declaring that the spirit or spiritual things are good, and the body or material things are bad. It's not hard to figure out why humans would want to make peace with the separation between the spirit and the body—it is a seriously traumatic separation, and its ultimate expression is death. There's something inside of us that knows that death is not, ultimately, good. And, through the lens of Gnosticism, sex, with all of its physical, sensual, and emotional power, is seen as bad. To be spiritual, to be "holy" is to be beyond sexuality.

iii. By the fifth century, St. Augustine wrote, "I know nothing which brings the manly mind down from the heights more than a woman's caresses," and "I HAVE DECIDED that there is nothing I should avoid so much as marriage."

iv. By the sixth century, Pope St. Gregory the Great wrote "the pleasure itself (sex) can by no means be without sin." By the sixth century, the most important teacher in the church was teaching that there was no way to have sex without sinning!

v. We actually see the end result of this gnosticism today when we behold an ultimate separation between sex (the physical, seen reality) and gender (the felt reality and desires, or the "spiritual") rather than seeing each human as a unified whole, valuing the language of sex that each body speaks. This separation was presented by Sigmund Freud (not a Christian), but happily taken up by many Christian communities who sought the security of safely defined "masculinity" and "femininity" as the idea of gender completely separate from male and female bodies.

vi. We crave meaning, beauty, and significance, which means that lists of "do's," "don'ts," and "because God said so's" are not—and never have been—enough to satisfy the longings of the human heart.

Slide 6 – Two Paths of Failure

If we follow the world to the end, we will find that...

i. Obsession leads to the pursuit of ever-increasing dopamine hits that ultimately do not satisfy. Sex remains meaningless, disconnected, and addictive. Standard porn doesn't get you excited anymore so it needs to be more and more exotic. We are trapped by the law of diminishing returns.

ii. Reductionism leads to long-term broken relationships with our own bodies, the people we use in order to get our own needs met, and with God who created us.

Slide 7 – Rules without meaning or the hope of healing lead to:

i. Shame, silence, and becoming trapped in a cycle: Try, fail, feel shame, seek isolation, repeat;

ii. Being disconnected from our God given desires and failing to enter into the joy and blessing of being created as sexual beings.

Slide 8 – GOD HAS A BETTER PLAN

What if there were answers to the real questions like: What is the meaning of sex? Why did God create us as sexual creatures? Wouldn't it be better not to have all these confusing desires than to be set up to fail?

Slide 9 – Testimony

Slide 10 – TRUTH #1: God Created Sexuality

See Genesis 1:27–31. God created humanity in his image as Male and Female. And when God saw what He had made, he described it as VERY good. This was the only time God used "very good" in all the days of creation, and it was in reference to humanity, body and soul, as distinct from one another yet reflecting His image *by their very sexuality*. This was God's plan, and it was the crowning event of all creation.

Sexuality is a term that encompasses maleness and femaleness, masculinity and femininity, sexual desire and attraction, physical intercourse and intimacy, biology, physiology, psychology, emotions, and—YES—spirituality. You cannot separate your sexual life from your spiritual life: it's all connected. They are meant to reinforce each other.

Slide 11 – TRUTH #2: Sexuality Reflects God's Image

Genesis 1:27 states that the first man and woman were created "in the image of God." Sexuality is unity in diversity, as in the Trinity. Father, Son, and Holy Spirit are all one God and yet three persons. Male and female are both fully human yet are individual expressions of that humanity. This is one of the highest pursuits of all philosophical inquiry. E Pluribus Unim. Uni-versity (unity-diversity).

Sexuality is rooted in the nature of God who is a community of persons: One God, three persons. St. Augustine referred to the Trinity as The Lover, the Beloved, and the Love between them. Father—Son—Holy Spirit.

Sexuality reflects the Trinitarian nature of God, the Father, Son, and Holy Spirit, who dwell in absolute and shameless intimacy, and create out of their great, self-giving love. This trinitarian picture is stamped on humanity: Husband-Wife-Conceived Child. Intimacy without shame. Vulnerability. Power. Pleasure. Sacrifice. Giving. Receiving.

So, what is the purpose of sex?

- God created sexuality (just like he created everything else) as a means by which we could experience His great love for us.

- Sexuality is a window through which we see God.

Slide 12 – TRUTH #3: Sexuality Declares the Gospel in Our Bodies

A. The gospel, the "good news", encompasses Jesus Christ's incarnation, ministry, death, resurrection, ascension, and then the coming of the Holy Spirit at Pentecost.

True Sexuality...

- Is unifying: it maintains and preserves difference, but leads to unity;
- Is voluntary and free: mutual giving and receiving;
- Is pleasurable: in giving we receive;
- Is total, unreserved and vulnerable: we give all of ourselves;
- Is fruitful: it has the potential to produce new life.

For this reason a man shall leave his father and mother and be united to his wife, and they shall become one flesh. (Gen. 2:24)

The Apostle Paul, in chapter 5 verses 31–32 of his letter to the church in Ephesus, was quoting Genesis 2:24 when he wrote: "'For this reason a man will leave his father and mother and be joined to his wife, and the two will become one flesh.' This is a great mystery, but I am speaking about Christ and the church.'" Jesus is the Bridegroom. The church is the bride. He is the one who left His mother and His Father's house. God, in Jesus, laid down His divine rights to cling to humanity. He is forever human. The two (God and humanity) have become one flesh in the body of Christ.

B. Sexuality is at the heart of the gospel.

A twisted understanding of sexuality leads to a twisted understanding of God and His plan for mankind.

There's more to sex than mere skin on skin. Sex is as much spiritual mystery as physical fact. As written in Scripture, "The two become one". Since we want to become spiritually one with the Master, we must not pursue to kind of sex that avoids commitment and intimacy, leaving us more lonely than ever–the kind of sex that can never "become one". There is a sense in which sexual sins are different from all others. In sexual sin we violate the sacredness of our own bodies, these bodies that were made for God-give and God-modeled love, or "becoming one" with another person. Or didn't you realize that your body is a sacred place, the place of the Holy Spirit? Don't you see that you can't live however you please, squandering what God paid such a high price for? The physical part of you is not some piece of property belonging to the spiritual part of you. God owns the whole works. So let people see God in and through your body. (1 Corinthians 6:16–30 MSG)

Slide 13 – TRUTH #4: Embracing Our Sexuality Honors God and Leads to the Abundant Life

A. Our powerful sexual drives are intended to propel us into relationships with God.
B. There is a profound difference between desire and sin. CS Lewis famously stated: "Our desires are not too strong, but too weak."
C. So, what is sexual sin?

Slide 14 – 1 Corinthians 6:13–14 (NLT)

You say, "I am allowed to do anything"—but not everything is good for you. And even though "I am allowed to do anything," I must not become a slave to anything. You say, "Food was made for the stomach, and the stomach for food." (This

*is true, though someday God will do away with both of them.)
But you can't say that our bodies were made for sexual immorality. They were made for the Lord, and the Lord cares about
our bodies. And God will raise us from the dead by his power,
just as he raised our Lord from the dead.*

Slide 15 – 1 Corinthians 6:15–20 (NLT)

*Don't you realize that your bodies are actually parts of Christ?
Should a man take his body, which is part of Christ, and join
it to a prostitute? Never! And don't you realize that if a man
joins himself to a prostitute, he becomes one body with her?
For the Scriptures say, "The two are united into one." But the
person who is joined to the Lord is one spirit with him.*

*Run from sexual sin! No other sin so clearly affects the body
as this one does. For sexual immorality is a sin against your
own body. Don't you realize that your body is the temple of
the Holy Spirit, who lives in you and was given to you by God?
You do not belong to yourself, for God bought you with a
high price. So you must honor God with your body.*

Slide 16

Not inviting God into our sexual experiences is sin. Engaging in sex
that violates God's pattern for sexuality, which reflects His image, is
sin. So, sinful sexual expressions and actions are those which are not
free, total, faithful, or fruitful.

Slide 17 – TRUTH #5: Sexual Wholeness Is Possible

A. God gave you desires. All desires at their root are from God, many
   desires are simply distorted or bent. Meet Jesus in your desires
B. We have God's Spirit. It is actually possible to begin to see people the
   way Jesus sees them.

C. You can exercise your will. Healing and Empowering and exercising the Will.

D. Confession to another breaks the power of shame. When you experience temptation, brokenness, even sin, are you able to invite Jesus into that?

Slide 18

God wants to heal us even more than we want to be healed. The healing of our sexuality looks like:

i.   Freedom from the power of lust - being able to love as a selfless and generous giver, rather than lust as a consumer;

ii. Freedom and healing from the rage, bitterness, fear, repression, and physical cost of past sexual trauma;

iii. Freedom to express sexual desires to a spouse without passivity or manipulation;

Slide 19

iv. Freedom from accusation, shame, demonic lies, and addiction surrounding my sex, and sexuality;

v.   Freedom to bring my sexual energy into all interactions and engage with women and men as sisters and brothers, not objects of lust, power, fear, and domination. Not needing to be afraid that we are like animals who can't help but have sex when left alone;

Slide 20

vi. The ability to trust God to realign my body and my desires into a unified whole;

vii. Freedom to be attentive to my desires, and allow them to be a part of a conversation of encounter with God.

Slide 21 – Instructions for Prayer

To break soul ties with past sexual partners:

- Identify hooks—traumatic or sexual memories, insecurities, images, or places that the enemy uses to yank us in the direction he wants us to go;
- Confess all sexual sin (see your Spiritual Profile if you need help);
- Forgive those who have used or abused you, release them to Jesus, and receive the justice and freedom which flows from His side.

Slide 22 – Renounce Any and All Shame

- Renounce passivity and manipulation.
- Receive hope, healing, and identity from God in every area of your sexuality.

Keys of the Kingdom

Slide 1 – Keys of the Kingdom

Slide 2 – The Gospel

Mark begins his story of Jesus by saying this: "Now after John was arrested, Jesus came into Galilee, proclaiming the gospel of God, and saying, 'The time is fulfilled, and the kingdom of God is at hand; repent and believe in the gospel.'"

Wait a minute. What is Jesus preaching? The gospel. What is the gospel? Here's where our evangelical background has failed us: usually we're taught that the gospel is that Jesus died on the cross in our place so that we can be forgiven and go to Heaven someday, right? That is a beautiful truth, but unfortunately that is only a piece of the gospel. What is Jesus saying the good news is? The Kingdom of God is at hand. What is the Kingdom of God? We're near the state of Maine, so this should be easy to remember: the Kingdom of God is the way life should be. First John 3:8 says the reason the Son of God appeared was to destroy the works of the devil, to undo the curse, to bring heaven to earth, to restore that which was lost in the garden.

- We have this small view of salvation that goes like, "I prayed a prayer when I was eight years old and just hang on friend, someday we'll make it to Heaven." Now there's nothing wrong with praying a prayer of salvation, but salvation is a gate. It's just a gate—a beautiful, glorious gate—praise God for this gate! But there is a whole kingdom to walk into! So many of us spend our lives sitting in the gate and we fail to walk into the good news that is the abundant life Jesus offers. It's what Peter mentions in his letter: "participation in the divine life." It's what John says in his letter: "as he is, so are we in the world."

What Jesus is calling us to do this weekend is to enter the Kingdom. How do we do that? Repent and Believe.

Slide 3 – Repent

Salvation is not a one-stop shop. To give your life to Jesus is like giving Jesus the title deed to your house. For the rest of our lives, *repentance* and *belief* are the acts of welcoming Jesus into each individual room and allowing Him to turn the lights on, clean out the garbage, and make His home in us. We welcome Him into the rooms of our traumatic and shameful memories, into the rooms of our addiction, pain, or bitterness. We invite Him into our personality and our relationships.

Remember our analogy from **The Four Rs**: Repentance is agreeing with Jesus that your favorite coat (sin) is actually bad. You won't take it off unless you believe it's bad, unless you see it for the lie it is and agree with the truth. Repentance allows us to continually encounter Jesus in every area of our lives. This is how we abide in Him and He in us.

Slide 4 – James 5:16

Confession to a safe, compassionate, but also clear-thinking person is powerful. The Bible speaks of it as a means of healing. So often, we are stuck in our own heads, and no matter how many times we confess to God and beg Him to take it away from us, the old thoughts, shame, and sin patterns return again and again.

The enemy of our soul loves darkness. Actually, he can only work in the dark. Confessing to another person by saying the sin out loud, by bringing another person into the conversation, is what John calls "walking in the light" with one another. "But if we walk in the light as he is in the light, we have fellowship with one another, and the blood of Jesus, his son, purifies us from all our sin" (1 John 1:7). The fruit of this practice is incredible. We are no longer the super Christians we want everybody to think we are. Instead, we are united by bonds of mutual love and sympathy as we stand before the cross together. We confess our sins one to another, and we repent before God, declaring our intent to live life differently from here on out.

Slide 5 – Renounce

Once we see an area of sin in our lives and repent before God, the next step is to renounce it. Why? We've already called it sin and are agreeing with God's truth. Why must we renounce it? **There actually is an enemy. There are real spiritual forces, not just bad ideas, that war against us and the Kingdom of God that is advancing through us.** Renouncing is not only calling the sin "sin," but declaring the truth, speaking it out to ourselves and all the powers of darkness. It is helpful to name all the lies you have believed surrounding this sin. This is why we often make a list (of people, of places, of events, of ungodly beliefs) and then destroy it later. The late Derek Prince, a long-time Bible teacher, said, "When the words we speak about ourselves agree with what God says about us in Christ, then we open the way for Him to make us in actual experience all that He says we are." We can learn to say to the enemy, "I hate you! I set my will against you. I break all agreements with you that this sin has brought into my life."

- We can be like David, who after he struck Goliath with a sling and a stone, marched over to him and cut his head off!

  So David triumphed over the Philistine with a sling and a stone; without a sword in his hand he struck down the Philistine and killed him. David ran and stood over him. He took hold of the Philistine's sword and drew it from the sheath. After he killed him, he cut off his head with the sword. When the Philistines saw that their hero was dead, they turned and ran. (1 Sam. 17:50–51)

- When Satan and his demons see that we have struck down pride or bitterness or unforgiveness or lying or gluttony or any other sin in our lives, **and** they hear us renounce it, then they will flee. To keep our freedom, we must often keep on renouncing the sin and declaring God's truth. We must be willing to obey the Spirit and forsake the old ways. The enemy WILL return to press on those areas he once held. In order to hold those rooms, that freedom, we must fill those rooms with something: encounter with God(!), truth, belief, infilling of the Holy Spirit, new practices, new ways of being, new ways of thinking, and new ways of speaking. We are changing the locks. We have received the new keys of the Kingdom with all of the access and authority of the King.

Slide 6 – Believe

Believe Jesus is the King. As Westerners, we are often deeply inclined toward democracy. But the Kingdom of Heaven is not a democracy: it's a kingdom. The way this Kingdom life works is by us allowing the King access to every part of our lives.

> *For through the law I died to the law so that I might live for God. I have been crucified with Christ and I no longer live, but Christ lives in me. The life I now live in the body, I live by faith in the Son of God, who loved me and gave himself for me. I do not set aside the grace of God, for if righteousness could be gained through the law, Christ died for nothing!* (Galatians 2:19)

The kingdom of darkness is on a serious budget, and some of the cheapest line-items are intimidation, lies, and shame, which lock us in patterns of passivity and unbelief. Jesus is not a thief. He will only take what you give Him. If you want to keep your shame, He will allow it, even to the deepest detriment of your relationship and life in God. He has given you that much dignity! We choose to repent and actually believe the good news.

Slide 7 – Isaiah 61

God the Father anointed Christ to bring us good news, to heal us, to give us liberty from those things that bind us and to walk in the freedom He purchased for us. This is our inheritance, our gift from Him. Jesus began his earthly ministry with this proclamation from Isaiah 61.

Slide 8 – Wholeness

We are all on a journey of wholeness and holy love. All of who we are must heal, grow, and respond to the goodness of God. "Jesus replied: 'Love the Lord your God with all your heart and with all your soul and with all your mind.'

This is the first and greatest commandment. And the second is like it: 'Love your neighbor as yourself'" (Matt. 22:37–39).

- Sin has a way of affecting our whole being. We must address sin and its effects on our whole selves.

- Our SPIRIT, once created to house the Spirit of God and bring the power and presence of God to us, was dead—lifeless– because of our independence from God and our embracing of sin. Once God regenerates it through the new birth, His Spirit comes and fills it again with His life. This is our new birth that takes place at salvation.

- Our SOUL (mind, will, and emotions): Although our spirits are regenerated and have come alive, our souls are bound by years of sinful habits and ungodly beliefs. We must learn to tear down the lies in our minds and take every thought captive to the obedience of Christ. (See 2 Corinthians 10:3–5.) We learn to "will" His will, think as God thinks, and feel in a wholesome, life-giving way. This is a process, a lifetime journey.

- BODY: We start seeing our body as the temple of His Spirit, a place that will reflect Him in every way and is made for many encounters with God. We agree with God that our bodies are a beautiful gift from Him and then we learn to worship God with our bodies. God starts healing us from sickness and disease and even from the effects of a reckless life.

Slide 9 – Jesus Is King

We need one another to persevere and press on to complete wholeness. This is a journey of going "further up and further in." We welcome the Kingdom of God in every part of us and in every part of our world as we repent and believe the good news. JESUS IS KING!

Include your testimony here:

- What have you been set free from? *Name the sin.*

- How did this impact your life? Relationships? Prayer? *Be specific.*

- How did you come to realize your need to repent?

- What did God do for you? How did you take authority over your mind, will, emotions, and body, coming into alignment with the kingdom of God?

Be Filled With the Holy Spirit

Slide 1 – Be Filled With the Holy Spirit

Good morning! It is with joy that we come together this morning anticipating all that the Lord has planned for us, His beloved (daughters/sons). We have seen the Lord move this weekend, forgiving our sin and shame and washing us clean with His love and healing our hearts. This morning we are going to talk about who the Holy Spirit is, and what it means to be filled with the Holy Spirit. Let's start at the beginning...

Slide 2 – Who Is the Spirit?

In the beginning God created the heavens and the earth. Now the earth was formless and empty, darkness was over the surface of the deep, and the Spirit of God was hovering over the waters. (Gen. 1:1)

In the formless and empty darkness, the Spirit hovered, waiting to bring new life and beauty into being. In perfect unity with God the Father, the creator, who through Jesus the Word would speak all things including you and me into existence, the Spirit moved to **bring new life, new creation**. The Spirit from before time has been bringing spectacular beauty out of chaos, brooding over darkness and emptiness, waiting to bring new life.

As we move through the pages of the Old Testament, we see the Spirit falls on particular people for particular tasks. **The Spirit gives a special anointing** to those chosen to make a beautiful dwelling place for the Lord in the Tabernacle, the place of worship for God's people. The Spirit comes upon the leaders of God's people to give them great **strength** for battle, **faith** in impossible situations, and **words of knowledge and prophecy**, especially about the coming Messiah.

As we have seen this weekend, sin costs us our freedom and brings darkness into our lives. This was the state of God's people, who had given their hearts over to their own desires and chosen idols over the living God. To His people, who were far from Him, God promises through the prophet Ezekiel,

> I will sprinkle clean water on you, and you will be clean; I will cleanse you from all your impurities and from all your idols. I will give you a new heart and put a new spirit in you; I will remove from you your heart of stone and give you a heart of flesh. And I will put my Spirit in you and move you to follow my decrees and be careful to keep my laws. (Ezek. 36:25–27)

This was the promise of the Holy Spirit—the promise of the New Covenant that was coming.

Slide 3 – "He will baptize you..."

In this place of waiting the Spirit comes upon a man named John. The angel Gabriel said before his birth that "he will be filled with the Holy Spirit even before he is born." John's calling was to "make ready a people prepared for the Lord." John called Israel to repent, to turn from sin, and to come to be baptized as a sign of saying yes to the promises of God. He was preparing the way for Jesus, the Messiah. But John told the people that when Jesus comes, there is going to be a different kind of baptism.

> I baptize you with water. But one who is more powerful than I will come, the straps of whose sandals I am not worthy to untie. He will baptize you with the Holy Spirit and fire. (Luke 3:16)

To Baptize means:

1. to dip repeatedly, to immerse, to submerge (like sinking of a ship)

2. to cleanse, to wash, to make clean with water

3. to overwhelm

The word baptism was used of vessels that were sunk, filled in every possible place with water. It describes being submerged, overwhelmed, filled to the very brink of fullness. John says *that when Jesus comes, you can expect to be baptized, or submerged with the Spirit, the Spirit of power.*

Slide 4 – "Let anyone who is thirsty..."

Jesus Himself spoke of the Holy Spirit, promising Him to His disciples and followers after His death and resurrection. He said:

> *"Let anyone who is thirsty come to me and drink. Whoever believes in me, as Scripture has said, rivers of living water will flow from within them." By this He meant the Spirit, whom those who believe in him were later to receive. Up to that time the Spirit had not been given, since Jesus had not yet been glorified. (John 7:39)*

Jesus actually told His disciples that it was good He was going away, just so they could receive the Holy Spirit! "But very truly I tell you, it is for your good that I am going away. Unless I go away, the Advocate will not come to you" (John 16:7).

Slide 5 – Born of the Spirit

Under the New Covenant, the Holy Spirit brings new life to every believer, fulfilling the promise of Ezekiel to give us a new heart and put a new spirit in us. This is what happens at salvation—being born again. As we become members of Christ's body, we receive a new heart and the gift of the Holy Spirit who never leaves us or forsakes us.

This is the new birth Jesus spoke to Nicodemus about in John chapter 3:

> *Jesus answered, "Very truly I tell you, no one can enter the kingdom of God unless they are born of water and the Spirit. Flesh gives birth to flesh, but the Spirit gives birth to spirit. You should not be surprised at my saying, 'You must be born again.' The wind blows wherever it pleases. You hear its sound, but you cannot tell where it comes from or where it is going. So it is with everyone born of the Spirit." (vv. 5–8)*

Slide 6 – Who Is the Holy Spirit?

Scripture teaches us many things about the Holy Spirit:

- He is the Lord and is to be obeyed (Acts 7:51)

- He is the Spirit of Jesus (Rom. 8:9)

- He reveals the secrets of the Father (Eph. 1:17)

- He convicts of sin (John 16:8)

- He is Helper, Counselor, & Comforter

- He gives direction (Acts 10:19–20, 13:2, 16:6)

- He saves us (John 3:3–7)

- He is our joy (Rom. 14:17)

- He intercedes (Rom. 8:26)

- He testifies to our spirit (Rom. 8:16–17)

- He grieves (Eph. 4:30)

- He empowers and gives courage (Acts 4:13)

- He helps us overcome sin (Heb. 10:29, Eph. 3:16)

Slide 7 – "I baptize you"

At salvation, the Holy Spirit baptizes us into the body of Christ. First Corinthians 12:13 says, "For we were all baptized by one Spirit so as to form one body—whether Jews or Gentiles, slave or free—and we were all given the one Spirit to drink."

The invitation this morning is for you to ask Jesus to baptize or fill you with the Holy Spirit. Just as He came upon those disciples who were waiting in the upper room at Pentecost, He will come to fill us today! Holy Spirit delights in bringing new things, new attitudes, new desires, new ways to pray and to worship. His desire is to make Jesus known and transform us into Christ's image. We need to be filled and refilled so that we might see God for who He really is, and who we really are in Him. God has created us to be the very temple of the Holy Spirit (1 Cor. 6:19)!

It is hard to say "Yes" to being filled with the Spirit without wondering a bit: "What does that mean? What is going to happen?" So, what does it mean to be filled with the Holy Spirit?In Matthew 3:11, John the Baptist says, "I indeed baptize you with water unto repentance, but He who is coming after me is mightier than I, whose sandals I am not worthy to carry. He will baptize you with the Holy Spirit and fire."

In his book, *The God I Never Knew*, Robert Morris paraphrases John's statement like this: "You've seen me immersing repentant people in water, but I am just a forerunner for the much greater One, Jesus, who will immerse reborn people in the fire of the Holy Spirit."

And this statement of John appears in all four Gospels: Mark 1:8, Luke 3:16, and John 1:33.

Who is doing the baptizing in these verses? It's Jesus!

What is He baptizing us in or with? The Holy Spirit!

Jesus told his disciples to wait in Jerusalem until they had received this baptism. In Luke 24:29, Jesus says " I am going to send you what my Father has promised; but stay in the city until you have been clothed with power from on high." And then as the Book of Acts opens, we read, "On one occasion, while he (Jesus) was eating with them, he gave them this command: "Do not leave Jerusalem, but wait for the gift my Father promised, which you have heard me speak about. For John baptized with water, but in a few days you will be baptized with (or in) the Holy Spirit."

See Robert Morris, *The God I Never Knew: How Real Friendship with the Holy Spirit Can Change Your Life*. WaterBrook Press, 2011. 183–185.

Slide 8 – What Does the Holy Spirit Do? (1)

What does the Holy Spirit do?

• He brings about our adoption as daughters of the King (Rom. 8:14–16).

• He makes us more like Jesus (2 Cor. 3:16–18).

- He gives good gifts to those who ask (Gal 5:22–23; 1 Cor. 12:4–11).

  Fruit of the Spirit, Wisdom, Words of Knowledge, Healing, Miraculous Power, Prophecy, Discernment, Prayer Language, Interpretation of Tongues

Slide 9 – What Does the Holy Spirit Do? (2)

- He grants a prayer language and the ability to prophesy (Acts 2:2–4, 14–21).

- He fills every empty place, as He brings into being new life in us (Acts 2:21).

  But whenever anyone turns to the Lord, the veil is taken away. Now the Lord is the Spirit, and where the Spirit of the Lord is, there is freedom. And we all, who with unveiled faces contemplate the Lord's glory, are being transformed into His image with ever-increasing glory, which comes from the Lord, who is the Spirit. (2 Cor. 3:16–18)

Slide 10 – The Holy Spirit Brings:

Here are just a few of the benefits and blessings that friendship with the Holy Spirit brings:

- **Comfort:** Jesus called the Holy Spirit the Comforter, and He is a constant presence in our lives, ready and able to infuse us with peace and assurance (John 14:15-17; 1 Cor 14:3).

- **Counsel:** The Holy Spirit is the Counselor who leads us into all truth and shows us things to come (John 16:13; Acts 16:6).

- **Fellowship:** The Holy Spirit is an ever-present companion and friend who just happens to be God! (2 Cor 13:14; Phil. 2:1).

- **Prayer Help:** The Holy Spirit is ready and available to help us pray more effectively and to actually pray through us (Rom. 8:26; 1 Cor 14:15).

- **Power:** The power to be effective witnesses, to be bold, to understand the Bible, and to pretty much do everything the Christian life is supposed to involve comes from the indwelling, Holy Spirit (Luke 24:29; Acts 1:8, 10:38; Rom. 15:13; 1 Thess. 1:5).

- **Liberty.** True freedom is a work of the Holy Spirit in our lives. It's a work we must authorize and cooperate with (Rom 8:2; 2 Cor 3:17).

And there's so much more!

See Morris, 183–185.

Slide 11 – Good Gifts!

When we are filled with the Spirit, we receive good gifts, for the Holy Spirit loves to give them to anyone who asks for them! "But the fruit of the Spirit is love, joy, peace, patience, kindness, goodness, faithfulness, gentleness and self-control" (Gal. 5:22–23).

> Now to each one the manifestation of the Spirit is given for the common good. To one there is given through the Spirit a message of wisdom, to another a message of knowledge by means of the same Spirit, to another faith by the same Spirit, to another gifts of healing by that one Spirit, to another miraculous powers, to another prophecy, to another distinguishing between spirits, to another speaking in different kinds of tongues, and to still another the interpretation of tongues. All these are the work of one and the same Spirit, and he distributes them to each one, just as he determines. (1 Cor. 12:7–11)

Today, ask for one of these gifts from the Father!

Picture the disciples, having seen Jesus taken back up into heaven, sitting together anxiously in prayer together. They had prayed for ten days, waiting with anticipation for the word of the Lord to come to pass. And then it happened, and the Spirit fell. Scripture says it was like this:

> *Suddenly a sound like the blowing of a violent wind came from heaven and filled the whole house where they were sitting. They saw what seemed to be tongues of fire that separated and came to rest on each of them. All of them were filled with the Holy Spirit and began to speak in other tongues as the Spirit enabled them. (Acts 2:2–4)*

It says some people were amazed and many were bewildered. It says they were perplexed, asking "What does this mean?" Some people made fun of them, saying "They have had too much wine." This is good news! The supernatural does not always make sense in the natural. Today, as the Holy Spirit moves you may feel amazed, bewildered, maybe a bit perplexed, and you too may ask, "What does this mean?" As you experience the Lord today, you can trust that He is good. He gives good gifts to His children and loves to delight those whom He loves.

In this place of amazing bewilderment, Peter stands up and addresses the crowd, and says,

> *Fellow Jews and all of you who live in Jerusalem, let me explain this to you; listen carefully to what I say. These people are not drunk, as you suppose. It's only nine in the morning! No, this is what was spoken by the prophet Joel:*

> *"'In the last days, God says,*
> *I will pour out my Spirit on all people.*
> *Your sons and daughters will prophesy,*
> *your young men will see visions,*
> *your old men will dream dreams.*
> *Even on my servants, both men and women,*
> *I will pour out my Spirit in those days,*
> *and they will prophesy.*
> *I will show wonders in the heavens above*
> *and signs on the earth below,*
> *blood and fire and billows of smoke.*

> *The sun will be turned to darkness*
> *and the moon to blood*
> *before the coming of the great and glorious day of the Lord.*
> *And everyone who calls*
> *on the name of the Lord will be saved.' (Acts 2:14–21 NIV)*

This is what we are invited to today! We are invited to say yes to the promise of the Father, to all that He has for us. We are invited to receive an anointing of the Holy Spirit. This is the One whom Jesus promised.

Slide 12 – Hindrances to Being Filled

There are hindrances to being filled: unrepented sin, fear (distrust of God, fear of man, loss of control), complacency and pride, or the lack of a poor spirit (Matt. 5:3), lack of asking (James 4:3), doubt (Luke 11:9–10).

There are often things that prevent us from being filled with the Holy Spirit. If you are struggling with any of these this morning, come for prayer!

Slide 13 – Testimony

Include your testimony here:

- What hindrances did you have that kept you from knowing and experiencing the Holy Spirit?

- How did this impact your life? Relationships? Prayer? *Be specific.*

- How did you encounter the Holy Spirit?

- What did the Holy Spirit give you? How were you filled?

Slide 14 – Come!

This morning, "The Spirit and the bride say, 'Come!' And let the one who hears say, 'Come!' Let the one who is thirsty come; and let the one who wishes take the free gift of the water of life" (Rev. 22:17). Come! Are you thirsty this morning? Are you ready to receive the water of life, the infilling of the Holy Spirit? Are you ready to let Jesus baptize you with the fire of His Holy Spirit? Come!

Run With the Vision

Slide 1 – Run With a Vision

Slide 2 – The Vision of Encounter

The Vision of Encounter
for you to run with personally and invite others into.

"To see people set free by the power of the Holy Spirit and released to walk in the fullness of their identity as men and women created in the image of God."

- The *end* and the *beginning.*

- Encounter is more than a weekend.

- This weekend, the scales have come down and you have seen God for who He really is: not angry, not like your father or mother, not distant and unconcerned, but ready to encounter you, to show Himself and His love to you.

- Encounter is about coming to know God.

- When we encounter God, we learn who we are.

Slide 3 – Who Am I?

Names: You came here this weekend with names given to you by others, by yourself, that were possibly based in the evil one's lies, or that clung to you because of sin.

- You have come to the cross and you are leaving with a new name/ new identity.

New Name: God is not going to fix up the old. He died in the place of the old you. The old you was far too messed up to fix, and so He killed it. He invites you to leave the old you dead. You don't have to ever resurrect the old you, because He died so you could be free of it.

But what does it look like to *be* the new you?

- President of the USA

- Pastor Friend

- What does Monday look like as _____?

(Point of examples: you have to learn what it looks like to live as the new you.)

Slide 4 – Peter

Peter:

- received his name before he actually lived it outhad to hunger for Jesus

- had to continually receive from Jesus

- had to believe that what Jesus said was true

- had to learn to see himself the way Jesus saw him

- had to learn to interact with others, not as the old Peter, but as the new Peter – the rockhad to learn to walk in trust, and we see him open himself to everything Jesus had for him as he willingly received the Holy Spiritwas set free to live a life of love and power.

The heavenly reality spoken by Jesus came to be a physical reality as Peter grew in confidence and knowledge of his identity and mission.

Freedom:

- This weekend is about freedom. You have been set free.

- You are set free to live into your new identity.

Slide 5 – You Have Taken Off Your Old Self

You have "taken off your old self with its practices and have put on the new self, which is being renewed in knowledge in the image of your Creator."
What does it look like to be the new you? What does tomorrow look like?

- It is going to be a battle.

- Today is a feast, tomorrow is a battle.

Isn't it amazing that we are loved by the God that promises to set a banquet feast in the presence of our enemies? He will fill you in the midst of the battle.

Slide 6 – So How Do You Stay Free?

So how do you stay free?
St. Paul puts it this way...

"It is for _freedom_ that Christ has set us free. _Stand firm_, then, and do not let yourselves be burdened again by a yoke of slavery."
Galatians 5:1

But how do you stay free?

- There are things we need to do in order to keep living in freedom.

- It's not that God would take our freedom away, or that our freedom wouldn't still be available even if we sinned. Our freedom has been secured. Guess what? You are going to sin again when you leave this place. But Christ has died for every sin you did in the past, the present, and yes, even in the future. Let that sink in: He already knows and has already paid for you to be free of every sin you have yet to commit. You are free of your future sin, right now and forever.

- The battle has been won by Jesus outside of us, but the battle inside, the **battle of the mind**, often continues to rage,.

- The battle is waged against **strongholds, or lies** that we have believed about God and believed about ourselves.

- A stronghold can be a way of thinking about God that is so utterly unworthy of who God really is and how He really feels about us that it leads us *away* from Him instead of *to* Him.

Slide 7 – Stand Firm

- Roman infantry shields were full-length. They stretched from head to toe and were secured to the soldier's arm. The soldiers would stand shoulder to shoulder with their shields up and interlocking with each other. Behind the first line, a second and third row of soldiers lifted interlocking shields to rest atop their helmets, creating an impenetrable roof.

- They would step forward at the same time at the same pace. If the legion in this formation met opposition from an advancing horde, they would meet the opposing force with their shield wall.

- The first line would lean back into the second and third lines which would hold them up as they pressed into the oncoming enemy.

Slide 8 – Roman Battle Formation

What Paul calls the "belt of truth" was a very large and very thick leather belt buckled extremely tight about the waist and lower abdomen – like the belts used by body builders. It was especially useful to strengthen and reinforce the abdominal core in order to stand.

Slide 9 – Advancing Against and Attacking a Stronghold

- To stand, therefore, was not a primarily defensive but rather an offensive tactic to ward off attack by making an impermeable defense while advancing against a stronghold.

- To stand was an offensive posture: it was not passive.

- We must actively engage in the battle if we are to stand firm as we seek to tear down strongholds in our minds that have kept us from encountering the real God as opposed to the God of our broken imaginations.

Here are some things you need to take away from these images:

- **You are going to have to do something to keep your freedom.** You cannot just go home and hope for the best. You are heading into a battle, and no battle is won without some strategy.

- If your strategy is "me and Jesus," you are going to get seriously beat up.

- **IT IS IMPOSSIBLE TO GO IT ALONE**. Why? Because God didn't make you that way. Period. His Word on the matter is this: "It is not good for man to be alone." He made us to need one another as we stand in His truth.

Slide 10 – Live Out of Your Identity

Live out of your IDENTITY

- **Press in to the <u>knowledge of God</u>**
- **The "4 R's"**
  - —Repent
  - —Renounce
  - —Release
  - —Receive
- **Walk in the Light**

We want to send you home with some real weapons against the evil one:

- **The knowledge of God:** Psalm 27:4 says, "One thing I ask of the LORD, this is what I seek: To gaze upon the beauty of the LORD and to seek Him in his temple." The beauty of the Lord refers to seeing God and His true nature and heart toward you the way it actually is. There is absolutely no room for shame in our relating to God. We must begin to recognize the strongholds in our own minds and allow Jesus the room to demolish them all by his Spirit. When you spot shame, chances are you have found Satan's latest hiding spot.

- **The 4 Rs:** Repent, Renounce, Release, Receive. Practice this by yourself and with other people. Do it tomorrow morning, just because. This is a weapon you can wield against the evil one every day.

- **Walk in the Light:** Practice regular confession and prayer with one or two others, preferably with those who you believe to be "further along" in their journey with Jesus.

- Some of us need an entirely new paradigm of how to do "church" and "Christianity" to live into our new freedom. We need a new wineskin that will hold the new thing God is doing. This new wineskin includes living confessionally and receiving (as well as learning how to give) prayer ministry regularly with like-minded believers who will call you higher. It means regularly engaging in the practice of the supernatural gifts of the Holy Spirit in community for mutual edification.

- If you come from a church community that does not openly function this way, trust the Holy Spirit. Do not try to convert your whole church this week. Jesus says that new wine in an old wine skin causes the skin to burst. Let's agree together to not burst any wineskins, OK?

- Find one or two other believers who will walk with you, who will pray with and for you, who will listen to what God is saying and will encourage you to live it out.

- *Stop and pray for God to provide for each person what (who) they need. Interlocking shields – we are dependent upon one another's faith, to extinguish the fiery darts of the enemy.*

Slide 11 – Live in to Your Mission

Live in to your MISSION

- Your testimony – say it loud!
- Jesus' mission is YOUR mission too – Is. 61
- Find out what God is doing and join Him there
  – this is obedience.
- Find a safe place to practice

- **Your testimony – say it loud.** In the areas of your life where you've been set free, you now have authority to set others free. The same things you've been delivered from or healed of, you now have authority to deliver others and heal others of in the name of Jesus. God wants to release your testimony as a weapon against the enemy and the hopelessness he has spoken to those in bondage.

- The mission of Jesus is also YOUR mission.

> *The Spirit of the Sovereign* Lord *is on me,*
>   *because the* Lord *has anointed me*
>   *to proclaim good news to the poor.*
> *He has sent me to bind up the brokenhearted,*
>   *to proclaim freedom for the captives*
>   *and release from darkness for the prisoners,*
> *to proclaim the year of the* Lord's *favor*
>   *and the day of vengeance of our God,*
> *to comfort all who mourn,*
>   *and provide for those who grieve in Zion—*
> *to bestow on them a crown of beauty*
>   *instead of ashes,*
> *the oil of joy*
>   *instead of mourning,*
> *and a garment of praise*
>   *instead of a spirit of despair.* (Isaiah 61:1–3)

- Look for what God is doing and JOIN him there!

- Find a safe place to practice and live out what you have received. If you don't find a safe place to be involved with healing ministry and discipleship on a regular basis you will waiver, spin your wheels, and become complacent.

Slide 12 – Testimony

Slide 13 – "We are never visited..."

"We are never visited with a healing or deliverance, which we can then safely forget. Grace is not a pill we are given, or a method applied to us so that we can simply go on about our business. Grace always invites us forward. Every liberation requires continued attention, every healing demands continued care, every deliverance demands follow-up, and every conversion requires faithful deepening.

Slide 14 – "If we do not respond…"

"If we do not respond to these ongoing calls, if we deny our empowerments for continued growth in freedom and responsibility, our healings may well be stillborn. Then, as in Jesus' words about evil spirits returning to a house swept clean, our last condition may turn out to be worse than our first."*

Do not leave today without a plan. How will you engage the battle? Think right now of who you are going to call and call them on the way home. Invite them to walk with you.

* Gerald May, *Addiction and Grace: Love and Spirituality in the Healing of Addictions*. New York: Harper Collins (1988), 155.

Ways Encounter Culture can support you:

Slide 15

- **Kingdom**: You have a new mission; you need some competencies to live it out. Come learn how to do the things that Jesus did.

- **Encounter**: Encourage your friends and family to come to the next Encounter.

- **Encounter Builder**: Join a year-long coaching cohort and learn how to bring the ministry and lifestyle of Encounter Culture to your community.

God loves to call that which is not as though it were, He lives to bring beauty from ashes, and restore all things. He is committed to the full restoration of his image in you and has given you a number of ways to engage him in this beautiful restoration – will you join him there? Will you stand firm and live into your freedom? Will you allow him to finish what he has started in you?

Made in the USA
Middletown, DE
16 October 2023

40535854R00126